TECTONICS OF PLACE II

THE ARCHITECTURE OF JOHNSON FAIN

TECTONICS OF PLACE II

THE ARCHITECTURE OF **JOHNSON FAIN**

CONTENTS

SELECTED WORKS

FOREWORD

MICHAEL WEBB

A common thread runs through the varied work of Johnson Fain. One might call it poetic pragmatism: a respect for practicalities, context, and the environment, enlivened by flights of invention. The firm's steady growth, in scale and the range of typologies, is based on its ability to resolve every challenge and satisfy discerning clients, but there is always something more. Computer software allows architects to realize their wildest fantasies, but Johnson Fain employs it with restraint, to inflect rather than distort their buildings. And a sense of history grounds this work while enriching its modernist vocabulary.

They first made their mark with tall buildings. A century ago, Bruno Taut proposed a Stadtkrone: a skyscraper that would rival the great cathedrals as the dominant feature of city skylines. Now that all large cities boast a dense cluster of high-rises and a few vie to have the world's tallest, a notable tree is often lost in the forest. But the office and apartment towers of Johnson Fain excel in grace more than height and have become singular markers. Museum Tower in Dallas borrows the idea of entasis from classical columns, and the horizontal thrust of its bowed balconies plays off the verticality of a sheer curtain wall. It holds its own in a parade of arts buildings by Pritzker laureates.

All of the firm's towers, in the US and Asia, reject the stereotypical straight shaft, by animating the base, sculpting the profile, and turning facades into a geometrical tapestry. Some rise from a landscaped podium or treat the rooftop as a gathering place for occupants, a shaded belvedere in which to enjoy the cooler hours of a tropical day. Paired towers contrast with each other or are linked in a fraternal embrace. Johnson Fain looks back to the creative achievements of the pioneers, for whom Louis Sullivan penned "The Tall Office Building Artistically Considered," and forward to the latest energy-saving materials and technologies, while infusing these sleek structures with humanity.

That concern for residents, users, and passers-by—a rarity in the field of commercial development, where profit is the dominant concern—becomes even more apparent in those categories of building where people come first. Nowhere is that more evident than in the First Americans Museum outside Oklahoma City, which symbolizes the return of land, disfigured by oil extraction, to the tribes that hold it sacred. This fusion of architecture and landscape is an expression of culture, a repository of its artifacts and narratives, and an inspiring work of Earth Art, immersing visitors in a world of timeless values. Christ Cathedral in the Southern California community of Garden Grove has similar goals. A soaring glass shed that served as an evangelical television studio has been transformed into a Roman Catholic cathedral where space and light are subtly modulated. A volume that formerly had all the spirituality of a convention center has become numinous, a place of awe even for non-believers.

Johnson Fain was challenged to create an ideal work environment for two of the world's largest biotechnology companies: a tightly organized solution for Genentech in South San Francisco and a landscaped campus of low-rise labs and offices for Amgen in Thousand Oaks on the outer fringe of Los Angeles. In that expansive complex, sand-toned facades, pergolas for outdoor meetings, and generous plantings domesticate cutting-edge research and make best use of a benign climate.

Miguel Contreras Learning Center responds to urgent needs in a densely populated district of downtown Los Angeles. It relieves pressure on local schools by offering classrooms for 1,700 students, mostly from poor immigrant families, and recreational facilities for the entire district. Of necessity, it's a tough, heroically scaled structure, clad in corrugated metal to withstand hard use. Structure and services are exposed within the lofty interiors, and the vibe is that of a workshop, a no-nonsense place for shaping and enriching lives.

Well-planned, affordable housing is in critically short supply in major American cities, nowhere more so than in Los Angeles, where rents are skyrocketing, and homelessness has risen to shamefully high levels. LA Plaza Village is a new community in the heart of downtown, stepping down a slope to El Pueblo, the cradle from which Los Angeles grew. Graphics and vibrant colors draw on the Hispanic heritage of the area. Close by, Blossom Plaza is enlivened with scarlet balustrades and lanterns to provide a visual link to Chinatown. And the same exuberance is found within Guild Lofts, a crisp foil to the red brick warehouses of the former Navy Yard in Washington, DC. These three developments reinforce the existing genius loci; in the Runway at Playa Vista and at Citrus Commons in the San Fernando Valley, the architects have created a sense of place where none existed.

In the wine country of Napa Valley, Scott Johnson returned to his roots. "I grew up in the Salinas Valley, surrounded by the soft folds of the hills that turn golden in summer," he recalls. That love of nature is evident in the way that the Opus One Winery is rooted in the land, while paying homage to the past in walls of rusticated limestone and a rotunda in the spirit of Claude-Nicolas Ledoux. It has now been extended to provide more space for production and hospitality, using steel, glass, and wood to create an understated foil to the monumentality of the original. By contrast, the Byron Winery in the Santa Maria Valley of California abstracts the rural vernacular of a barn.

Four of the residences featured here were designed by Scott Johnson for his family and each is a radically different response to specific sites and evolving needs. Box House was built when his children were small and evokes a simple cabin, refined, multiplied, and extended to embrace a panorama of wooded hills that reminded him of his own childhood. The Larchmont Boulevard townhouse is compact, metal-clad and inward-looking, fitting comfortably into a busy commercial street. Wall House is clad in Corten steel to protect it from fire, to insulate the west facade from summer heat, and to evoke in its rusty brown surface the trunks of the trees that frame it. A linear sequence of rooms opening onto a pool incorporates a central gathering place that doubles as a stage for intimate concerts. Detached studios for painting and dance, and a pergola for outdoor activities complement the main structure. Most recently, a converted loft, conveniently close to the firm's downtown office, has replaced the townhouse as a snug base for empty nesters.

Large and small, public and private, rural and urban: these varied projects were created by a talented team of architects, engineers, landscape and interior designers, guided by seasoned principals, but all bear Johnson's personal stamp. His commitment to modernism is free of ideology and displays an affection for legacy, materiality, rigor, and the occasional romantic flourish. Nothing is willful or superfluous. These are purposeful buildings that manifest the enduring virtues of firmness, commodity, and delight.

INTRODUCTION

SCOTT JOHNSON

In 2010, the publication *Tectonics of Place: The Architecture of Johnson Fain* documented the major architectural projects of the practice until that time. Since then, more than a decade has passed and the firm's work has evolved with many new projects just as the criteria by which most architecture is commonly judged has evolved; the language of architecture is changing. A broad recognition of climate change and the need for sustainable practices, resilience in the wake of irregular weather patterns and potential destruction, social justice, and inequality have all cast architecture in a new light. Additionally, viral health, safety protocols, and the continued advance of digital communications have transformed our workplaces. Dense and occasionally abstruse, critical theory imported from adjacent fields has subsided and there is a new enthusiasm for building and the related arts that involve making things.

If familiar with our earlier architectural monograph, the reader will note that this second volume, following the first by over a decade, is a sequel entitled Tectonics of Place II and while the meaning of "tectonics" has perhaps not changed in the interim, the term "place" has not proved so durable. Tectonic, according to the Oxford English Dictionary, has its origins in archaic Greek and pertains to all the building arts taken as a whole, design through execution. Making its way into Latin and then into English in the 17th century, the term reappeared to describe "construction in general; constructional, constructive: used especially in reference to architecture and kindred arts." These meanings still seem relevant today as we are generally referring in this book not to an architecture of theory per se, but an architecture that is both conceived and then built with all its "kindred arts" in service to real world conditions. Consistent with the definition of tectonics, we are developing new technologies that conceptualize and produce architecture seamlessly.

The term, "place," however, may well be undergoing a migration away from physical space toward other meanings much like Silicon Valley's appropriation of "architecture" to describe software and the urban sociologist, Manuel Castell's reference some time ago to the "space of flows." While we remain mindful of the unique and place-specific qualities with which new architecture must dialogue, place has become freighted with alternative meanings leading to possible redefinitions. What is place

now in a world of digital and remote communications, virtual presences, artificial intelligence, and augmented reality? A "sense of place" as we used to call it, is now experienced in other dimensions. Still, we focus on the ways one chooses to build, what built objects say about the values of the work and who is served by the work. Architecture in our view is not an autonomous process as argued by an earlier coterie of critics and practitioners. To be architecture, the work aspires to a kind of inventive and intelligent language of building which is ultimately used to communicate and serve.

Notwithstanding the inevitable specialization that comes with certain commercial markets, it should be said that interior design at Johnson Fain is practiced as interior architecture. Our studio leader in that area of the practice has always been a trained and accomplished architect and we believe that, while the practice addresses specific issues that architecture may not, the most successful interior design is seamless with the architecture that embodies it.

This book selectively references a number of our earlier projects in order to clarify design lineages, from earlier to later work, where we believe they exist and to display how particular design elements and strategies evolve over time to address new conditions. While a project's impact stands on its own, as a historical event, it may be a part of a longer trajectory of design evolution. The majority of the work in this monograph, however, describes work completed in the last decade or currently under construction. Although each building is unique in its own way and a wide range of building types are represented, those exhibited here have been organized around broad topics to emphasize the underlying and central purpose of the work.

TALL

Tall buildings have always been a constant in our practice. In fact, the research that accompanied the many high-rise buildings of Johnson Fain spawned a trilogy of books on the building type, notably, Tall Building: Imagining the Skyscraper (2008), Performative Skyscraper: Tall Building Design Now (2014), and Essays on the Tall Building and the City (2017).

Our predecessor firm, William L. Pereira Associates (WLPA), had designed a number of high-rise buildings in its time, however, the tall buildings of Johnson Fain came online later, when different and specific critiques characteristic of the day were being promulgated. Our tall building designs attempted to address those issues. Evolving out of a critical period when postmodernism, a simplified title for a neo-historicist and rhetorical design approach was being replaced by a return to a broader legacy of modernism, another simplified title for a complex phenomenon, our early work attempted to bridge a number of those critical postures. Three tall buildings were built in sequence in Los Angeles' Century City, namely, Fox Plaza

Tall Building Imagining the Skyscraper

Performative Skyscraper Tall Building Design Now

Essays on the Tall Building and the City

Fox Plaza (20th Century Fox Headquarters), Century City, California

(20th Century Fox Headquarters, 1987), 1999 Avenue of the Stars (later, SunAmerica Center, 1991), and Constellation Place (MGM Headquarters, 2003). The Nestle USA Headquarters in Glendale, California and Rincon Center in San Francisco were also built among an assortment of unbuilt projects and garnered the attention of project sponsors in other cities and abroad.

Notably among these, we designed and oversaw the construction of Museum Tower in Dallas, a tall elliptical building that received both accolades for its architecture and notoriety for its adjacency to Renzo Piano's Nasher Sculpture Center. The city had long earmarked the site for a tall building but when, during construction, the building's glass curtain wall began to reflect sunlight into the Center's clerestories that had been directed toward the site by the building's architect, concerns arose. Following two years of photometric research on our part leading to a range of alternative solutions, the Center was unpersuaded to take action. Eventually, the consternation ran out of steam once it became clear that those who could address the problem were unwilling and Museum Tower was celebrated and proved to be among the premier residential high-rises in Dallas. We were fortunate as were others in the Arts District to be the beneficiaries of the large and ever-popular Klyde Warren Freeway Park fronting us and a host of important cultural buildings nearby designed by excellent architects.

Following some years working in China, Southeast Asia, and the South Pacific, we were commissioned by a prominent Indonesian developer to design a twin tower residential complex in Jakarta named Verde Two. Weather, street traffic, and security issues among many others led to the design of an extraordinary project with elaborate tropical outdoor recreational spaces and indoor social amenities. A commission for a twin tower residential project named Solitaire in the garden city of Taichung on the island of Taiwan led to a series of iconic towers for Pao Huei Development, a real estate and construction company located there. Meticulously constructed, finished, and furnished, a number of these buildings were located in the Seventh District, the cultural core centered around Toyo Ito's Opera House while others were at the city's expanding edge.

We have enjoyed opportunities over the years to propose high-rise buildings in Japan, the People's Republic of China, and Southeast Asia, and our endeavors led to completed projects in Jakarta and Taichung. We found that in both locations, sophisticated clients were capable of translating our architectural intent and detail with precision. Construction quality was high. Just as we were traveling abroad to visit them, they were traveling to the West to observe design trends and strategies far from their own markets. They wove important threads that were familiar, and in many cases highly aesthetic, from their own cultures into their work and adapted new ideas to their own context. Residential environments abroad are more culturally specific than work environments, which tend to be governed by more global physical

SunAmerica Center, Century City, California

Constellation Place, Century City, California

Nestle USA Headquarters, Glendale, California

Rincon Center, San Francisco, California

standards. Many of these included private access to residences; multigenerational living patterns; culinary traditions that require the redesign of kitchens, storage, and dining; as well as the selection of furniture, finishes and relevant artwork.

After some success in the US high-rise office markets that were very active until the 1990s and faded due to an oversupply of financing and product, the market for high-rise buildings turned to multi-family residential towers both for sale and for rent. That pattern has again been reinforced domestically throughout the 21st century due to broad housing shortages, the migration of residents to employment opportunities and amenities in the city centers and, more recently, the high vacancies in office towers due to pandemic-induced remote working which has slowed the demand for new office towers.

The urban design and planning studio at Johnson Fain had been providing site planning services and density studies for Mitsui Fudosan America (MFA), a Japanese multi-national corporation with a US division, for two long-held downtown Los Angeles sites. One of those sites, centrally located on Figueroa Street in the heart of the Financial District, became MFA's first candidate property for development and we were commissioned in 2016 to design a 42-story apartment tower on the site. As is the case with most high-density projects in Los Angeles, the automobile parking requirements are still sufficiently generous that once a builder maximizes the below-grade parking, a need still exists for additional parking above grade. The Planning Department and City Council, as in many cities, became critical of real estate developers' typical response to urban above-grade parking with its exterior ramps, flat concrete slabs and perimeter of cars, headlights, and the visibility of interior fluorescent lighting. In response, project teams began to build parapets shielding some of this and then added semi-transparent screens, louvers, and meshes to the exterior in order to clad the structures while allowing sufficient openness for ventilation and natural light to the interior. Ultimately, amid widespread dissatisfaction with all these strategies, the agencies came to require completely sealed garages, mechanically ventilated with high-quality architectural skins and taller flat clear ceiling heights with the hope that one day future transportation technologies would reduce self-driving and these large structures could be converted to other uses such as residential, retail, or work environments.

Johnson Fain's transition from office high-rise to residential high-rise has been an important one for us. Fortunately, we have enjoyed the sponsorship of some of the most committed real estate developers who operate at the top of their markets and take seriously the potential impact of architecture, the central role that landscape and amenities play in an urban lifestyle and the many particulars that must be designed into a vertical residence in order to accommodate a full spectrum of residential activities. Additionally, most of our clients are fully supportive of measures that need to be taken to reduce a project's carbon footprint and achieve higher levels of sustainability.

Museum Tower, Dallas, Texas

Verde II, Jakarta, Indonesia

Solitaire, Taichung City, Taiwan

Nantun, Taichung City, Taiwan

As all architects begin again to rethink the future office environment in the wake of the "creative office," the mobility and proliferation of digital devices and health protocols stemming from the recent Covid pandemic, Century City Center has been our most recent opportunity to proactively revisit the traditional model for the vertical workplace environment. Having the benefit of a long-term relationship with Chicago-based JMB Realty Corporation for whom we've designed two prior office towers and are now designing another, it is easy to measure how dramatic the differences are in Century City alone, by looking at our earlier buildings, their priorities, and our current project. The exterior of our new tower has been designed with each elevation articulated differently in relation to its incident solar exposure in an attempt to reduce cooling loads. An interactive two-acre garden atop a low-rise parking structure with indoor/outdoor social lounges, conference center, and gym complement a host of conveniences and support retail. With regard to equitable access, mobility, and the region more generally, the project is sited atop a major underground Metro subway station that delivers passengers to its front door. The project is targeting LEED Platinum certification.

CULTURE

Among the most interesting works engaging the office over the years are projects that constitute various cultural forms including religious communities, museums, educational institutions, government agencies, and centers of science and technology. These projects speak to the norms and belief systems of each group and they vary widely. As such, they have provided us valuable insights into the ways in which affinity groups form, the rituals they share, and how they choose to project their identities to the outside world.

An early project that expanded the theater and arts programs at the Marlborough School for Girls in Los Angeles allowed us to participate in the area of youth arts education that ultimately extended into the Los Angeles Unified School District, the second largest public school program in the United States. We were thereafter commissioned to design the Roy Romer Middle School in the San Fernando Valley and the Miguel Contreras High School in downtown Los Angeles. Those led to institutions of higher learning with the Sutardja Dai School of Engineering at the University of California at Berkeley and Cal IT^2 at the University of California at Irvine. Both of these buildings were programmed to support the evolving trend in higher education that commingled students, engineering research, and private sector science in an effort to educate, research, and innovate while creating products that addressed specific societal needs.

A number of projects materialized in the wake of our being retained by the general contractor, Swinerton Builders, to provide design/build services for the Junipero Serra State Office Building in downtown Los

City Park, Taichung City, Taiwan

Sky Tower, Taichung City, Taiwan

Figueroa Eight, Los Angeles, California

Century City Center, Century City, California

Angeles. Formerly the Broadway Department Store located at the historic intersection of Broadway and Fourth Street and long abandoned by the company's expanding brand, the neoclassical 10-story structure was acquired by the State and plans were made to convert it to the central State Office Building for the City of Los Angeles. The effort was part of a policy at the time and initiated by Governor Pete Wilson to consolidate a majority of State offices under a single roof. The plan supported a larger strategy that looked to rejuvenate central cities, create more efficient interface between departments, and take advantage of public transit systems serving the office sites and historic investments in urban services and amenities. Completed in 2001, Johnson Fain was subsequently retained to design five sites at the east end of the State Capitol in Sacramento to accommodate the Departments of Education, Health & Human Services, and General Services. Comprising nearly a million and a half square feet of workspace, the project included childcare facilities, hearing rooms, and auditorium, retail, parking, landscaped open space, and an elaborate public fine arts program. In addition to the goal of exemplifying the policy of consolidation, the projects were oriented toward achieving high levels of sustainability and energy conservation. Soon after the project opened, the Department of Education building became the largest project in California to achieve LEED Platinum certification. The successful completion of the Capitol project led us to a commission to design the Solano County Government Center, a similar consolidation of multiple government agencies in historic downtown Fairfield.

Another unique form of community, the Catholic Diocese of Orange approached us in 2012 to reimagine the landmark evangelical Crystal Cathedral designed by Philip Johnson and John Burgee and built in 1980 in Garden Grove, California. The goal of conversion to an active Catholic cathedral, to be renamed Christ Cathedral, appeared challenging at the outset. An all-glass building designed as a worldwide televangelical Christian ministry provided streaming global content from its services every Sunday and became widely known for Reverend Robert Schuller's program, "Hour of Power." In addition to being a place of worship, the cathedral functioned as a television sound stage. It featured a tall ceiling, lighting grid, camera angles, generous natural light, and electronic and recorded sound for transmission. So different from the European legacy of dark stone basilican cathedrals, the building was flooded with light, without artificial cooling, and with considerable glare and sound reverberation challenges. In addition, the building plan was a shallow diamond not easily supporting the nave-centric processional worship characteristic of the traditional Catholic mass.

Our goal as we defined it was to find overarching solutions to the many technical problems without having them perceived as such, but rather to be seen as a further embellishment of the cathedral's inherent beauty. We devised a series of triangular translucent panels fitted into the squares of the structural space frame that modified glare and acoustic reverberation and gave the building reflective surfaces onto which artificial light could glow in the evening much like the shade of a lamp. The altar, predella, ambo,

Roy Romer Middle School, North Hollywood, California

Miguel Contreras Learning Center, Los Angeles, California

Sutardja Dai Hall, Berkeley, California

and cathedra were located at the rear of the sanctuary with pew aisles radiating inward toward the altar to accommodate procession.

News of Christ Cathedral's completion, as happened with other projects, led to additional commissions, in this case, Reality San Francisco, a young Christian congregation in San Francisco's Mission District. The substantial redesign of an existing building in the Mission District is currently underway.

Another unique, long-term project came to us in two cycles, first as a site selection, programming, and master plan effort, and subsequently as a commission to design the First Americans Museum in Oklahoma City, Oklahoma. The project was located on a 300-acre site two miles east of downtown Oklahoma City long known as one of Oklahoma's premier oil drilling sites. The land, adjacent to the Oklahoma River, was remediated and the master plan effort located a variety of facilities, sited the program, and identified building forms that emanated from a tradition of Indigenous American mound-building, conceived to protect native structures from floods.

Conceptually, the building's principle forms consist of two intersecting circular arcs, representing the "Encounter and Inclusion" of the Western European occupation. Primary building elements represent earth, fire, wind, and water and the museum building is sited on cardinal points in response to the sun's rotation in the sky. From the center of the Festival Plaza surrounded by the berm rising to a height of 90 feet, a visitor can see through to the setting sun at winter solstice as well as the ascending promontory walk representing a Native view of the "procession of life." At the intersection of land and built forms is the Hall of The People, an all-glass prism for the celebration of Indigenous American life, around which exhibition galleries, the FAMily Discovery Center, offices, services, and the Xchange theater are located. The elaborate and highly layered design represents the collaboration of many participants, among them Hornbeek Blatt, our local associate architects; Hargreaves Jones, the landscape architects; and the office of Ralph Appelbaum, our exhibition designers.

Over the years, we have enjoyed the experience of designing various recreational and social clubs. In the early 1990s, we master planned and designed buildings for a massive residential resort on Guam in the Mariana Islands for a major Japanese home developer, which included a wide range of social spaces, conference centers, and club houses among other building types. In Barbados, Dermot Desmond and his partners commissioned us to design the golf clubhouse facing onto the Green Monkey Course at the island's fabled Sandy Lane Resort, a favorite holiday spot for visitors from the British Isles and Europe. Locally, we redesigned and rebuilt the Wilshire Country Club in Hancock Park from the ground up and more recently completed the restoration and redesign of the Los Angeles Country Club in two phases, an august Georgian building originally designed and built in 1910 by Summer Spaulding, a legendary Los Angeles architect.

Cal IT^2, Irvine California

Junipero Serra State Office Building, Los Angeles, California

Capital Area East End, Sacramento, California

Solano County Government Center, Fairfield, California

COMMUNITY

Two of the nation's overarching trends intersect in the design of multi-family housing, namely, the urgent need for a greater quantity of, and more affordable, housing and the need to build it in urban areas where decades of investment in retail, services, recreational opportunities, and public transportation have created a fertile and more sustainable plan for it. In the early 2000s, after years of designing a roster of high-rise office buildings, we were invited to design residential towers here and abroad. While we embraced the opportunity to design vertical residences, they were different from the design of high-rise office buildings in nearly all respects except their height.

Structural systems, elevator cores, and the building codes that govern such construction may be similar, however, the size and configuration of floor plates vary widely due to the nature of vertical residences that tend to be repetitively stacked to achieve utility efficiencies and cellular rather than open planned and column-free as in office buildings where specific tenants and their requirements have not yet been identified during the initial design effort. While the contemporary office environment is becoming more informal and less office-like, it still lacks the detailed support functions of a private residence. Accordingly, most urban residential projects consist of a range of social, recreational, and cultural offerings located at the base of the building, the roof of a low-rise podium, or at the top of the tower to take advantage of dramatic views.

In our residential practice we have generally been commissioned to design three different building types and while they all attempt to address issues of urban living, they are very different physical typologies, each bringing with it particular opportunities and constraints. First, due to our history of high-rise office buildings and our familiarity with designing them, the engineering and technologies involved, we are frequently invited to design tall residential towers in the US and abroad. These tend to be either steel or ductile concrete frame buildings with centralized utility and elevator cores and exterior curtain walls or window wall systems. Second, we have designed a number of low- and mid-rise buildings that are also "noncombustible," generally meaning concrete frames with infill such as Metropolitan Lofts in Los Angeles and Guild Lofts in Washington, DC. Finally, and consistent with so much production housing in the US, we have designed high-density, low-rise, multi-family residential buildings that are commonly wood-framed, often sitting atop a concrete base. Wood framing is the lingua franca of most suburban housing today and has by now made its way into the city as a method of building relatively inexpensively and quickly. While much that has been built is of minimal architectural interest, we have found the building type flexible and highly adaptable to different site conditions and cultural contexts.

In the past we had generally avoided low and mid-rise opportunities that often fell into the suburban model of wood-frame production housing surrounding an enclosed recreational courtyard with parking below or adjacent. These projects exist everywhere in the US and are frequently designed to maximize revenues on a given site, stay within a limited construction budget, and orient themselves inward, providing little benefit to the outward-facing public right-of-way. As we entered the new millennium, a number

Christ Cathedral, Garden Grove, California

First Americans Museum, Oklahoma City, Oklahoma

Sandy Lane Golf Clubhouse, St. James Parish, Barbados

LeoPalace, Manenggon Hills, Guam

of large sites became available in Los Angeles that were strategically located near public transportation hubs, were in many cases, part of a larger neighborhood circulation network whose dimensions were such that retail and services could support that circulation and the project perimeter, enriching the public right-of-way with activity and porosity. These qualities drew us into a number of these high-density, low-rise projects that we continue to design today. No longer islands unto themselves, the opportunity to extend and enhance the public realm and increase the housing count in a given neighborhood remains our focus in these project types.

One of our first major opportunities was the design of Metropolitan Lofts for Forest City Development Company in the South Park neighborhood of downtown Los Angeles. An original Community Redevelopment Authority (CRA) site, MetLofts was designed to be a mid-rise Type 1 industrial loft-style building. Its primary structure was concrete with steel sash floor-to-ceiling window systems spanning from concrete floor slab to floor slab above. Wood floors ran throughout, and kitchens, dining space, and living rooms were open-planned to increase the sense of scale of the personal space. Common amenities included social lounges, a screening room, an indoor/outdoor gym, gardens, and a swimming pool. While public transit, ride-share and other modes of transport catch up, Los Angeles is still the auto-driven city it has been for a century. As such, an above-grade parking structure was embedded horizontally into the site so that a resident could walk out of a car at an upper floor and directly into a residence with no grade change.

Guild Lofts constituted a further development of the work at MetLofts for the same multi-national real estate developer, this time its site was located within the historic 50-acre Washington, DC Navy Yard on a tributary of the Potomac River. The master plan conceived of both recycling a number of large, mostly concrete and brick historic buildings as well as the addition of new and compatible buildings on the newly landscaped river's edge. MetLofts had taught us that industrial loft-style housing was not just a cult preference but that there was broad mainstream appeal to housing that had uncluttered open domestic space, simple modern finishes, open galley kitchens, and large casement windows to maximize light, air, and views. While comfortable, these residences did not enforce an overriding design style upon a tenant but rather invited personalization by way of their simplicity, openness, neutral finishes, and flexible lighting systems.

These two projects led us to Blossom Plaza for a third building with the same client in our downtown neighborhood adjacent to the Chinatown Metro Gold Line station. Two hundred thirty-five residences were to be arranged in a fashion that would facilitate pedestrian circulation and civic uses from Broadway through the center of the project and onto the rail platform. Then, as if to corroborate the adage that "all real estate is local," we were commissioned to design nearby LA Plaza Village, a two-block vertiginous site that extended a pedestrian paseo from Downtown Union Station, Los Angeles' principal transit center (Amtrak, Metro, MetroLink) and College Station, a five-and-a-half-acre project comprising five buildings opposite the 32-acre Cornfield Historic State Park and the same Metro Gold Line station.

Wilshire Country Club, Los Angeles, California

Metropolitan Lofts, Los Angeles, California

Guild Lofts, Washington D.C.

Blossom Plaza, Los Angeles, California

College Station designed for Atlas Capital Group was an extraordinary opportunity to explore a project of great scale and examine the vertical layering with which density can enrich the urban experience. Comprising over 700 residences on five and a half acres, Spring Street, the roadway that separates the project from the park, forms a broad curve that allowed us to design a faceted and curved facade some 700 feet in length. It's a dramatic gesture that unifies a project that is actually five buildings atop a two-story podium. Lower levels are designated for parking and public amenities and the podium roof, or third floor, becomes a generous garden deck accessible to residents.

Early on, Runway at Playa Vista for Dallas-based Lincoln Property Company represented an opportunity to master plan and design a ten-acre thoroughly mixed-use, low-rise, high-density community center within a much larger master-planned residential community. Centered around a core of above-grade rental housing, the ground level was characterized by small pedestrian-scaled streets and blocks, lined with retail, food, and entertainment amenities. Grocers, apparel tenants, restaurants, theaters, and child-friendly recreation populated the public right-of-way. As at MetLofts, automobile parking was embedded into the rear of the project as to not interrupt the continuity of pedestrian uses along the street frontages. A wide-ranging arts program distributed fine arts and murals throughout the project with a six-story wind structure created by the artist, Ned Kahn, draped over the central vertical circulation tower.

Much of the Post-World War II corporate, industrial, and retail construction in outlying suburban areas in the US has historically embraced a familiar pattern of dense low-rise construction surrounded by an expanse of surface parking. This is particularly true of much of Southern California in the 1950s through the 1980s. Density was low, land use zoning was often segregated by building type, and automobiles were the preeminent means of travel. By the end of the century, densities were being up-zoned, auto traffic congestion was common, and a dawning awareness of climate change, carbon and energy inefficiencies were influencing planning agencies to create new policies. Introducing mixed-use zoning, facilitating pedestrian and bicycle transit, and requiring the creation of publicly accessible and green open space became part of the civic agenda.

While Johnson Fain has been invited to master plan and design a number of projects that fall well within this category, Citrus Commons, the site of the former Sunkist headquarters building in Sherman Oaks in the San Fernando Valley is a flagship project incorporating these trends. IMT Residential retained us to preserve and adaptively reuse the original headquarters building as a home for creative entertainment and media companies. The abundant surface parking on the site was relocated to the basement and consolidated into two low-profile above-grade garages. This allowed two courtyard residential buildings to be designed with ground level retail, townhouses, a grocer, and an expansive landscaped parkway buffering an adjacent highway corridor. Now residents could move easily from residence to work to retail, and nearby neighbors could circulate through the project to the improved recreational edge of the Los Angeles River

College Station, Los Angeles, California

Runway at Playa Vista, Playa Vista, California

Citrus Commons, Sherman Oaks, California

that borders the south side of the project. An impenetrable super block from the 1960s is now being converted to a pedestrian-friendly network of sidewalks, open space, and streets.

CRAFT

The Opus One winery in Napa Valley's Oakville opened some 30 years ago, heralded at the time as an early example of global wine unions, of Old World craft meeting New World technology. The well-known California vintner, Robert Mondavi, and the Baron Philippe de Rothschild, the scion of a legendary European family and owner of Mouton Rothschild in Pauillac, France seemed to fit the bill. Carefully planted, tended, harvested, barreled, and blended, Opus One, in its inaugural vintage, was released at a price point more familiar to collectors of French First Growth wines than even the most highly rated California Cabernet Sauvignons. Gravity-fed, cellar-barreled, three years in French oak, the wine received accolades and the winery became a landmark destination in the Valley and one of the first in a class of cult California Cabernets. Some 25 years later, Johnson Fain was invited by the winery's next generation of vintners to return and design a major expansion.

The original building had been an architectural marriage of two traditions located in the Valley, but years had passed and the original founders were no longer with us. Still, the wine had maintained its quality and premier position in the global wine market. In an attempt to expand the winery's capacity without compromising quality, both fermentation tank space and barrel rooms were added. Given years of success, offices and operations had grown over time into less-than-ideal conditions and as more guests wanted to visit the winery, hospitality and tasting space was limited. Preserving the front elevation of the winery as originally designed and as the familiar public face of the winery from the highway, we expanded production and operations to the rear with new hospitality areas to the north, all tucked behind the original building and berm. Sanded limestone walls carried into the new tasting rooms as did rough-sawn wood ceilings, concrete and stone floors, black iron millwork, and an expansive glass wall looking out to Mount Saint Helena and the vineyards to the north. The original palette carried forward into the new spaces but were more trim and less decorative. Joan Behnke collaborated with us, consulting on furniture, fixtures, and artwork with our client.

Looking back some years following the original design of the Opus One Winery and in an expansionary mode, Robert Mondavi Winery (RMW) had pursued a number of mergers, domestic and foreign. Among them, they chose to purchase the Byron Winery, a 600-acre site in north Santa Barbara County from founder and winemaker, Byron "Ken" Brown. Ken had apprenticed with a number of well-known local wineries and had become an innovative Central Coast leader with a particular interest in Pinot Noir and Rhone varietals. Ken remained the principal winemaker while Mondavi managed the business and the brand. Much of the winemaking had been done at the time in a farming shed next to an adjoining highway and Bob Mondavi wanted a simple building for the essentials of the winemaking and tasting processes, grape delivery and

Opus One Winery, Oakville, California

Byron Winery, Santa Maria Valley, California

Aetna Springs, Pope Valley, California

crushing station, tank and barrel rooms without laboratory and offices. The winery would mark the center of the site, surrounded by vineyards and with a backdrop of the rolling hills characteristic of the California coastal region.

In the design process, Ken became enamored of the pneumatic jacks that were typically used to move aircraft and proposed that the tank room become a large open space with concrete floors whereby stainless-steel tanks filled with fermenting grapes and juice could be wheeled about effortlessly and flexibly from loading to barreling. We sited the building into the cross-section of the hill such that trucks could deliver grapes above the tank elevation and gravity flow of the wine could be achieved with the tasting locations on the floor level facing the vineyard below and beyond.

Meanwhile, back in Napa, now in the Pope Valley to the northeast, a consortium of developers and investors invited us to master plan a recreational community around which a clubhouse would be the central feature. It overlooked a historic nine-hole golf course, thought to be the first course on the West Coast to be re-designed by Tom Doak, the celebrated course designer. At Johnson Fain, we had a prior history of well-known clubhouses and a knowledge of early Northern California architecture. As it happened, Bernard Maybeck, the celebrated Bay Area architect, was the designer of many of the historic buildings on the site and we took cues from those buildings and his "brown shingle" work from the early 20th century.

The Great Wall Winery in Hebei Province, People's Republic of China, is a two-hour ride on the high-speed train from Beijing's Central Station to the eastern coast on the Yellow Sea. Above a large sloping vineyard of several hundred acres, a collection of aging industrial buildings from the mid-1980s had accumulated over many years and constituted the working winery, a subsidiary of China Foods Corporation (COFCO). Following tours of both European and California wineries, executives of the Great Wall Wine Company determined that in order to promote and grow their wine sector and increase domestic sales, they would require a Visitor Center with winery tour, dining, guest rooms, and banqueting for special events. A new Center would serve as a destination to educate the population regarding wine culture, culinary pairing, and agriculture. Additionally, it might conveniently serve as a seaside conference center for corporate and governmental gatherings.

While there are several regions within China that have longstanding wine histories, the culinary traditions have been generally supported with beer and distilled spirits. Wine protocols and a deep understanding of wine's distinctive properties has been largely unknown as it is in the West. Much of the wine made to date is what we would consider of unremarkable quality, but the Chinese are pursuing viticultural research aggressively and beginning to evolve the quality and diversity of their domestic wines. They are already engaged in a number of partnerships with well-known overseas consultants such as the peripatetic Michel Rolland of France.

Great Wall Winery, Hebei Province, People's Republic of China

Sandy Lane Golf Clubhouse, St. James Parish, Barbados

Knife Pleat, Costa Mesa, California

The Sandy Lane Resort in St. James Parish on the island of Barbados was built in 1961 and for years considered one of the premier destination resorts in the Caribbean. The property came up for sale in 1998 and was purchased by Irish investors including Dermot Desmond, an ambitious and well-traveled Irish businessman. Their goal was to rebuild the resort, and the three golf courses on the property, to the condition of its legendary past. The Green Monkey Course was considered the most expensive course ever built at the time due to its rocky terrain. Following a visit to Opus One, Dermot called to invite us to visit the resort and ultimately commissioned us to design a clubhouse for the course that he wished to be without precedent. Because the siting for the first and tenth tees and the ninth and eighteenth holes radiated from the top of the hill, we sited the building at the intersection with panoramic views of the beach and the Caribbean Ocean below. To take full advantage of the views and trade winds, we designed a radial lounge, deeply shaded but open-air in the direction of the view and the course. The majority of the exterior walls were white exterior plaster made up of crushed local limestone and a cement plaster matrix, a traditional Bajan building material used on early 20th-century homes and buildings of distinction.

Recently, a unique opportunity emerged when the chef, Tony Esnault and his wife and partner Yassmin Sarmadi, were invited to open a new restaurant in Orange County, California. Tony and Yassmin were the co-owners of two celebrated restaurants in downtown Los Angeles when the Segerstrom family reached out to them to establish a destination restaurant at the South Coast Plaza in a portion of the retail property tenanted by high-end fashion labels. Knife Pleat, taking its name from a feature of fine apparel, the restaurant opened with a Michelin Star and the interior was designed to support the visibility of refined food preparation with an open kitchen and comfortable indoor and outdoor seating. Access from the mall was controlled through large, patterned-glass panels and white onyx walls.

HOME

Over the years, we have taken on the design of a number of single-family homes. Generally, we have not sought them out with any urgency due to the complexity involved and the significant time and detail required to execute a unique and highly crafted home. Our first endeavor was a home for my family in the Mayacamas Mountains above Saint Helena in the Napa Valley and it was by any relative measure a simple structure on a cautious budget set in an extraordinary landscape. Wrapped in wide rough-sawn cedar planks, the exterior of the building resembled a cluster of boxes that stepped gradually down the hill leading to a long ramp of lawn, a swimming pool, and vineyard. Surrounded by native landscape, the boxes were occasionally pulled apart and glazed to capture transverse views of the landscape as one descended down the broad landings leading to the living room. The entire interior was fluid and open with the exception of bedrooms and bathrooms allowing for informality between shared spaces.

Arts Studio, Ojai, California

Bridge House, Rutherford, California

Frame House, Los Altos Hills, California

Following the completion of the house, Robert Lieff, a prominent San Francisco attorney, learned of the house after it appeared in various publications, including on the cover of Zahid Sardar's book San Francisco Modern. He called to ask for a tour, after which he commissioned us to design a house for him and his wife above the resort, L'Auberge du Soleil, in Rutherford on the opposite side of the Valley. The Lieff House employed a number of the natural and unadorned finishes of the St. Helena House but was configured to create two clusters of private spaces connected by a glass "bridge" that joined the two clusters and constituted the living/dining room. A long narrow swimming pool was elevated above the ground plane and protruded into the forest of scrub oak and tufa boulders.

After the homes were published in the Bay Area, Brad and Lucy Wurtz, a young technology executive in Silicon Valley and his wife, contacted us. Brad had recently purchased a historic mid-century modern home in Los Alto Hills designed decades earlier by the architect John Funk. The single-story home was in disrepair but showed great bones reminiscent of much of the Case Study homes of Southern California. Thoughtfully sited atop rolling hills, the house was framed in steel with broad panes of glass and an extravagantly long single-story elevation. The Wurtzes' vision was to restore the house and rebuild the interiors with natural and sustainable materials, radiant flooring for passive heating and cooling and maximum daylight and ventilation. Their young children needed spaces to play and additional bedrooms, so we extended the house while Nancy Goslee Power developed the gardens.

Sometime thereafter, we met with another great couple, John and Dede Gooden, who had been burned out of their home in the Malibu hills in one of the particularly fierce seasonal wildfires known to the region. Committed to the native landscape and the community of Malibu, the couple purchased a nearby site with a plan for a much larger house that would be fire-proof with space for their young sons. Because the house was high up on the Malibu range, the driveway met the house on the upper of two levels and we designed a dramatic curvilinear stair descending to the bottom of a skylit drum that encased the living room. The radial two-story perimeter was designed as floor-to-ceiling glass supported by thin steel piloti, which also supported the roof. The full expanse of coastline was revealed upon entrance. Dede asked for ocean views from nearly every room so the southern elevation was largely transparent and open while the upper arrival side was private and closed to view.

In 2015, Drew McCourt, a young technology and sports investor came to us and explained that he had purchased an existing property in the Trousdale Estates of Beverly Hills. High on the hillside, an undistinguished home from the early 1960s overlooked a dramatic view of the Los Angeles basin. After a number of discussions with Drew and an understanding of what he would need, we demolished the house to its footings and rebuilt a home with a similar footprint but an entirely different relationship between the interior and exterior spaces. Opaque and private on the uphill arrival side of the house, the rear elevation was designed with motorized all-glass sliding panels to allow the south-facing elevation to open up completely

Drum House, Malibu, California

Inside/Outside House, Beverly Hills, California

Larchmont Boulevard Townhouse, Los Angeles, California

to the rear yard and the view below. A broad canopy followed the roof lines of the house and guesthouse to provide shade for outdoor activities around the swimming pool.

Larchmont Boulevard is the village Main Street for Los Angeles' Hancock Park neighborhood. Some years ago, an urban site was vacated when a small house went up for sale, a house that had for years served as Charles Schulz's production studio for the nearby Paramount Studios animated features based on his longstanding comic strip Peanuts. Sixty feet by one hundred feet deep with five-foot setbacks, the steel-wrapped three-story townhouse fit snuggly onto the site. The ground level accommodated parked cars, storage of various kinds, a guest room, media/music room, a rear garden with summer pergola, and a south-facing garden for winter vegetables. A gravel garden in the front with a perimeter of dense ficus, a tree canopy, and an outdoor dining table occupied the front setback and gave the house privacy on the busy urban street. The second floor was open-planned with kitchen, dining, living areas, a swimming pool, patio, and master bedroom. Additional bedrooms and a study were located on the third level.

National Biscuit Company (Nabisco) Lofts, a registered historic landmark from 1925, was adaptively restored and converted into 100 live/work lofts in 2006. Formerly a West Coast headquarters for Nabisco, the building served as executive offices, bakery, and storage for the company at a time when railroad spurs laced through the industrial neighborhood and connected with the Southern Pacific and Santa Fe rail lines. Double-height ceilings with tall windows bringing natural light deep into the interior, wooden floors, and weathered brick walls were all desirable features for the conversion from a historic workplace to an urban residence.

Alternatively, twelve acres on a flat meadow floor surrounded by a dense halo of native oaks provided a near perfect location for a one-story home in the Ojai Valley. Built close to the ground with low stone planters reaching out into the natural landscape, a series of ancillary buildings intended to augment extended family activities on the site were added. The main house is sited on a cardinal north/south axis as are all the additional outbuildings and planters. One outbuilding encloses a guesthouse and dance studio, another a painting studio, and at the end of the southerly meadow an outdoor performance pavilion was designed and built. Low energy and low maintenance were instrumental in conceptualizing the buildings that include rooftop rain collection, photovoltaic arrays, and a west-facing rain screen system to insulate the house from solar radiation and heat.

Architectural projects of the firm continue to represent great diversity. In an age of increasing specialization, we find that rigorous design methodologies, ongoing facility with evolving digital tools, and attention to the particulars of program and client apply to all projects and guide the firm forward. Attention to these factors, we believe, can contribute to an environment of intelligence and beauty.

National Biscuit Company (NABISCO) Loft, Los Angeles, California

Box House, St. Helena, California

Wall House, Ojai, California

TALL
CULTURE
COMMUNITY
CRAFT
HOME

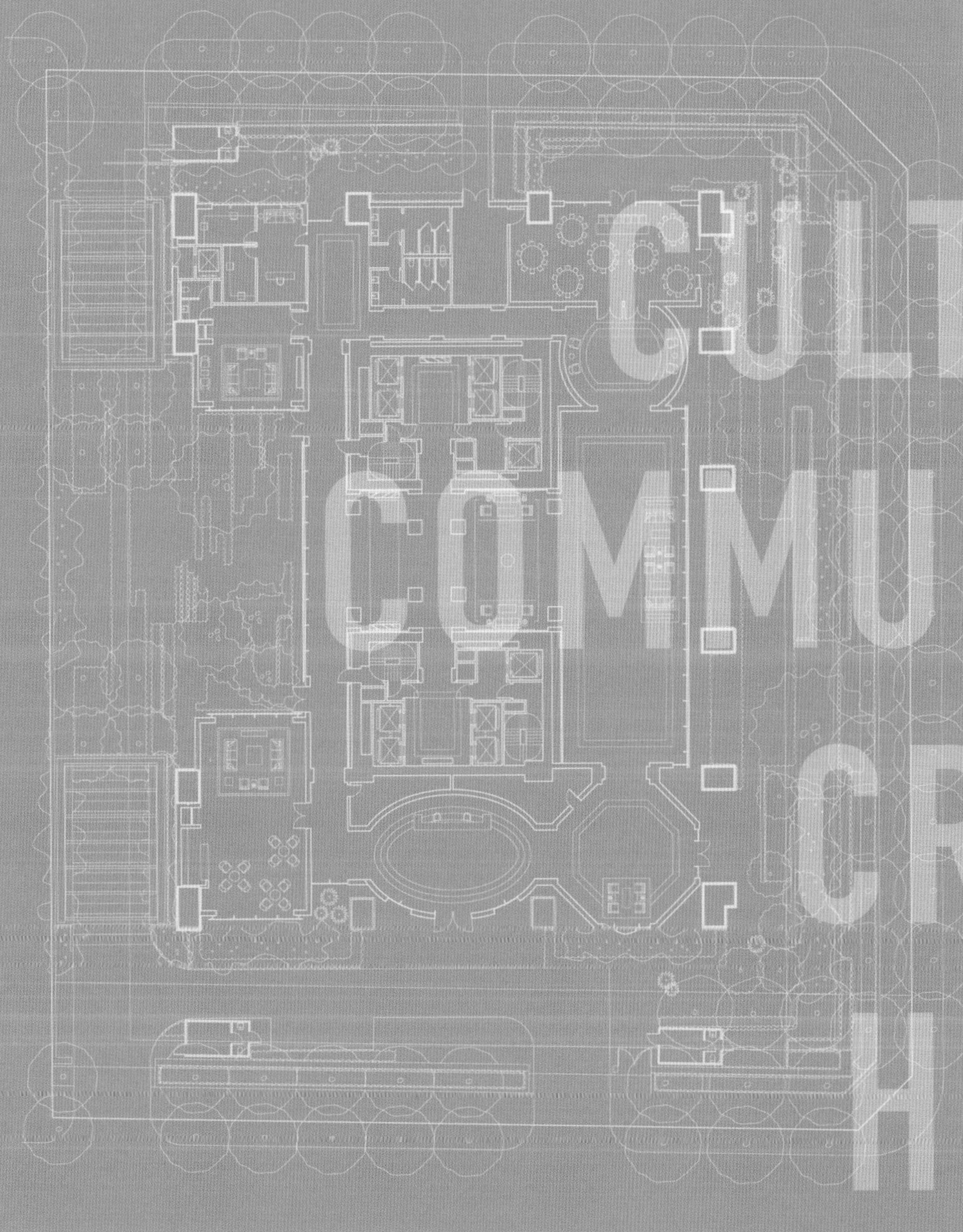

Located in the heart of the Arts District at the gateway to downtown Dallas, Museum Tower is surrounded by distinguished architecture and public open space. The project is sited among the Morton H. Meyerson Symphony Center, the Nasher Sculpture Center, the Dallas Museum of Art, and the Booker T. Washington High School for the Performing and Visual Arts. Fronting the Project is the three block-long Klyde Warren Park spanning the freeway and host to a wide range of public activities.

Museum Tower is a 42-story high-rise luxury condominium, providing 120 residences with secure below-grade parking and generous outdoor garden amenities. Individual residences are designed to take advantage of sweeping views of the city and beyond. An oval glass perimeter insures maximum natural light with elevators privately serving each dwelling. Outdoor sky terraces are located at the end of each floor, set deeply into the building to provide shade and sufficient outdoor space for furnishings and entertainment for each residence. Social and cultural amenities are available to residents at the ground floor including residents lounge and library, art gallery, and meeting space. A Wellness Center including fitness, personal services, yoga, exhibition kitchen, dining, and swimming pool are located at the second level. Museum Tower has received LEED Gold Certification.

MUSEUM TOWER
DALLAS, TEXAS

Sheraton

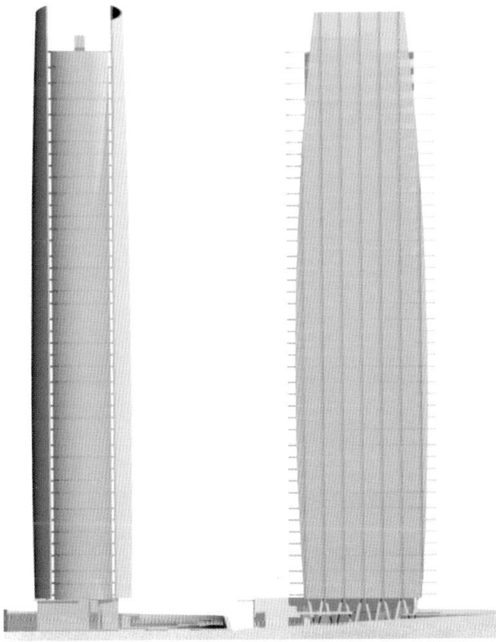

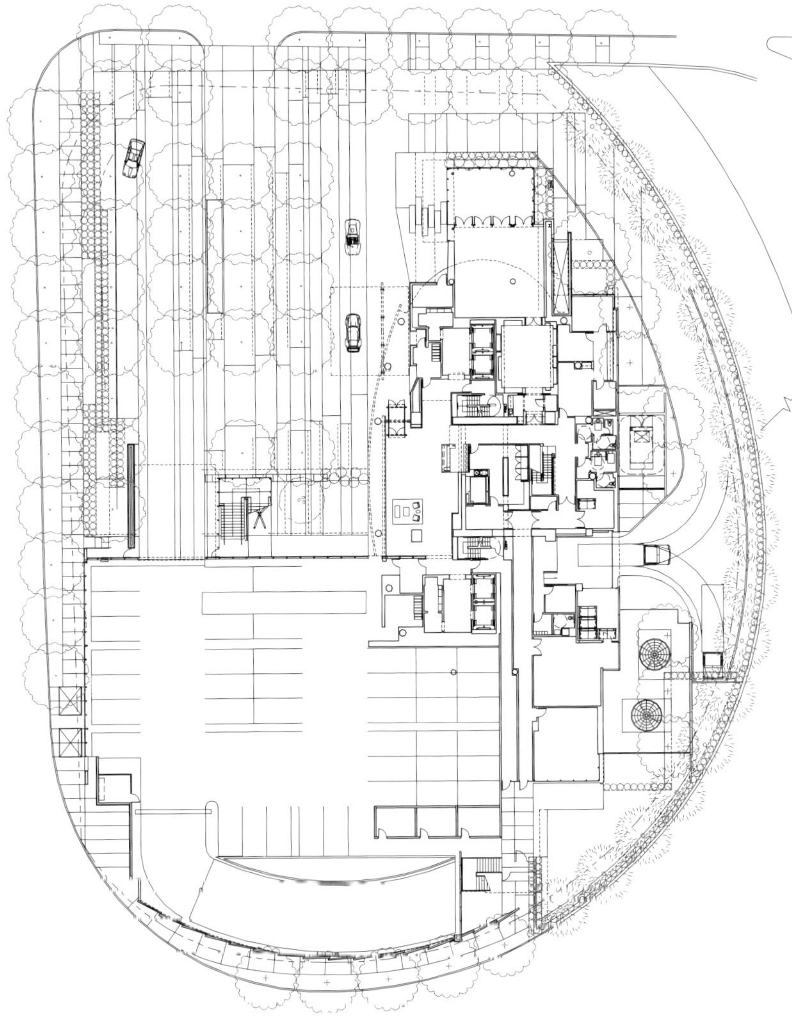

GROUND FLOOR PLAN

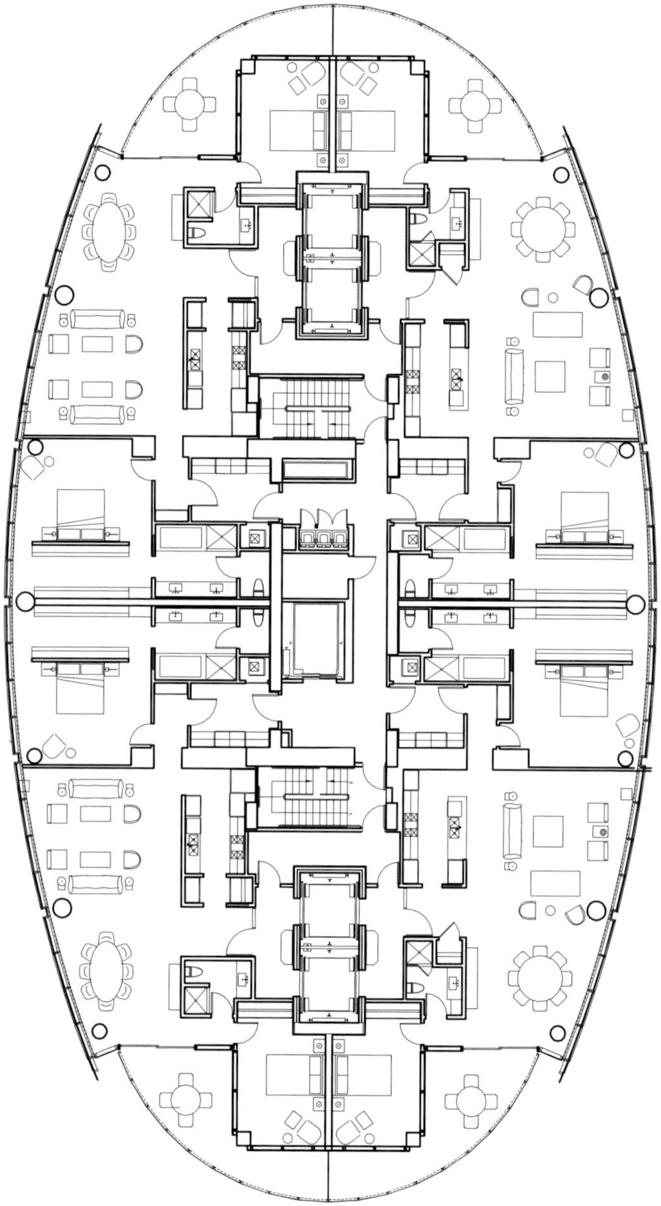

21ST LEVEL FLOOR PLAN

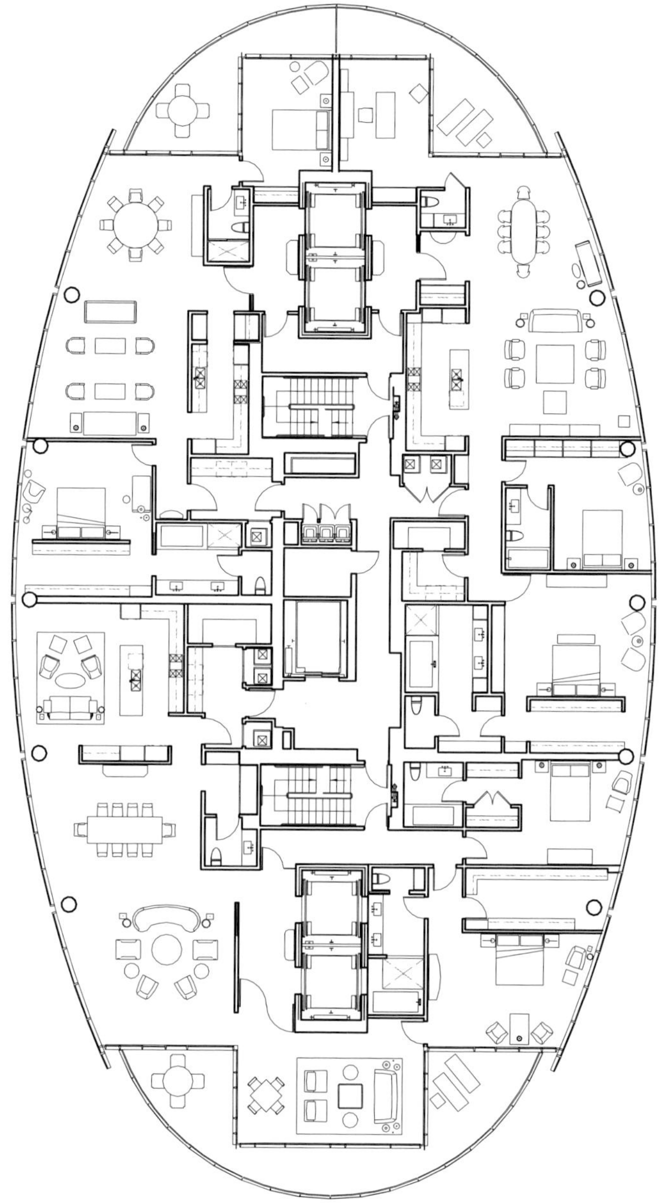

36TH LEVEL FLOOR PLAN

Jim Hodges
Hopper
DALLAS MUSEUM OF

This 37-story office tower is the newest tall building in Century City. Sited at the intersection of Avenue of the Stars and Constellation Boulevard and incorporating a major subway portal for the Metro D (Purple) Line, the project provides high visibility and easy access. A formal motor court for valet parking, retail amenities, and a large lobby to access the floors above make up the ground level. Atop the two-story parking podium is a two-acre publicly accessible garden with gym, meeting pavilions, conference center, and indoor/outdoor social lounge. The exterior architecture of the tower is designed with floor-to-ceiling high-performance glass with varying shading devices on each elevation responding to its solar orientation, reducing heat and the building's energy consumption. The project is targeting LEED Platinum certification, which would make it the leader among Southern California's commercial buildings.

CENTURY CITY CENTER
CENTURY CITY, CALIFORNIA

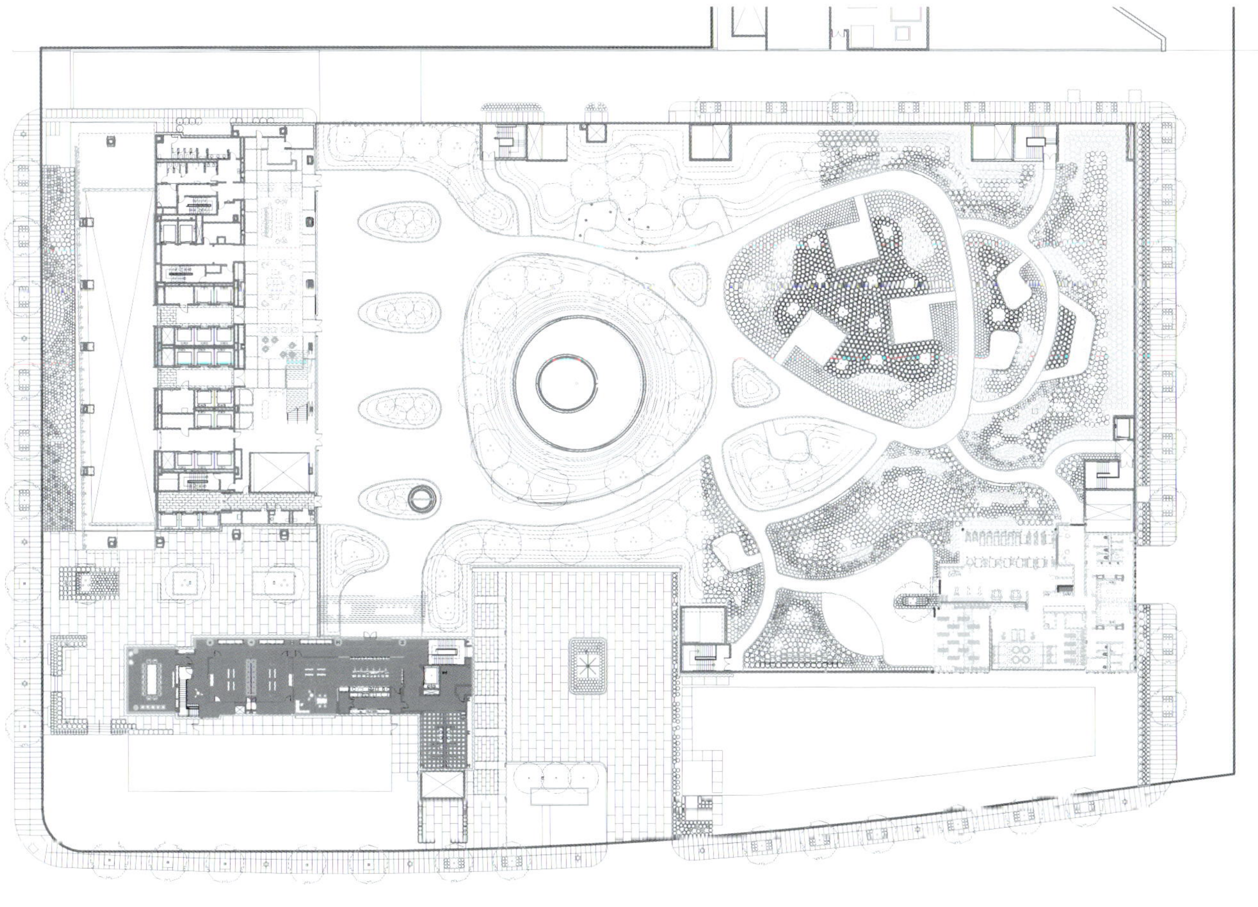

SECOND FLOOR PLAN / PODIUM DECK

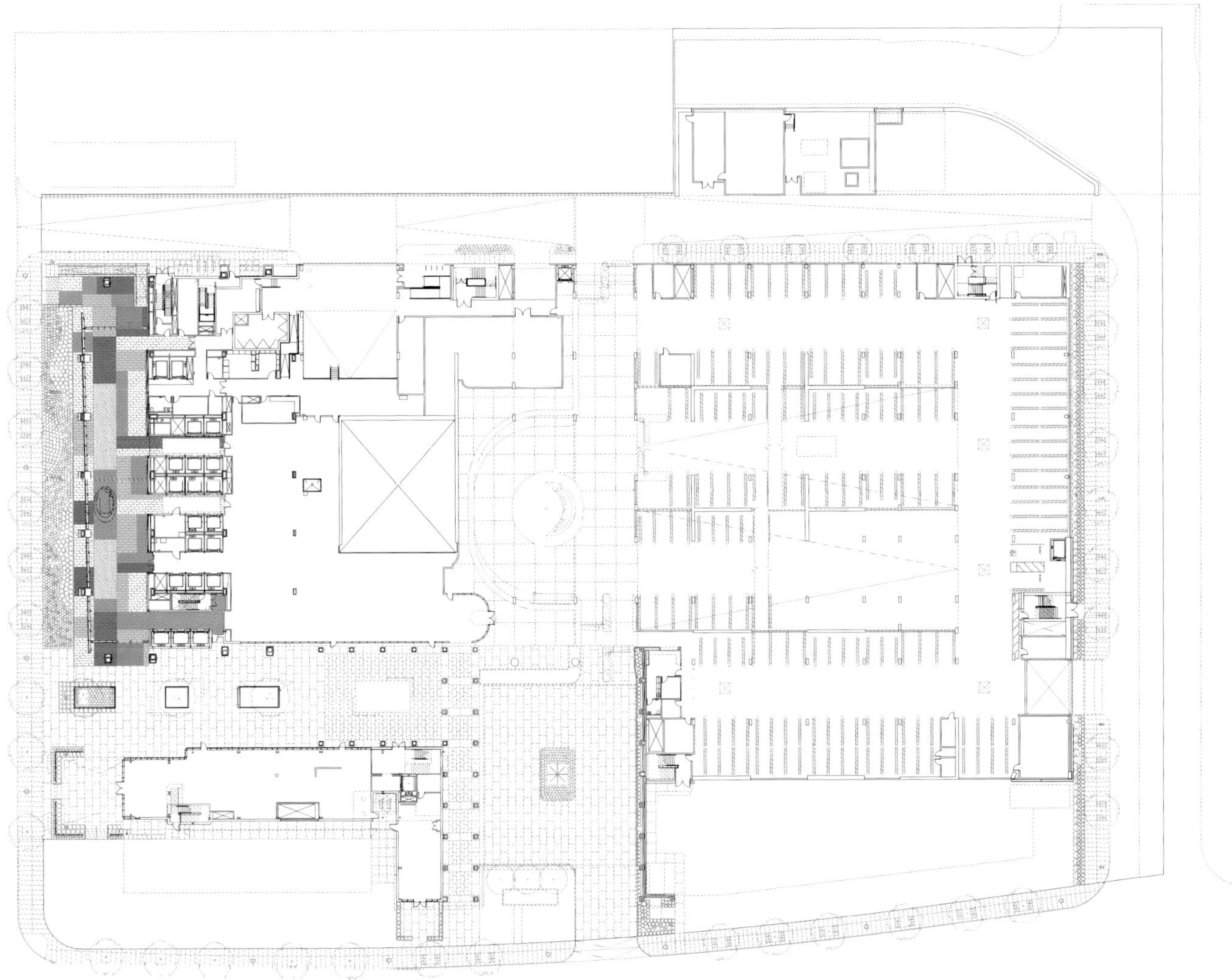

GROUND FLOOR PLAN

Johnson Fain designed a luxury condominium project comprising two 42-story towers located in Taichung City. Each floor contains two condominium homes that are approximately 3,100 square feet in size. Generously planned, each home enjoys high levels of security, personalized elevator access, spaciously scaled rooms, and balconies. Located one block from Toyo Ito's Metropolitan Opera House, each home has wide and tall expanses of glass with views of the opera house and plaza, the nearby civic park, and the dramatic skyline beyond.

The ground level of the towers is sited with a private motor court for automobile arrival. Surrounded by dense gardens and works of art, the ground floor includes a tall elliptical reception lobby, tea room, salon, library, lounge, and meeting rooms. Each room looks out into the lush garden environment. Private fitness, treatment, and social amenities for homeowners are located on the second level. Chief among them are a floor-to-ceiling glass interior containing a swimming pool and spa. On the top floor of the building, the two towers are joined to create one super-floor with spectacular views and providing residents with a Sky Lounge and Banqueting Center.

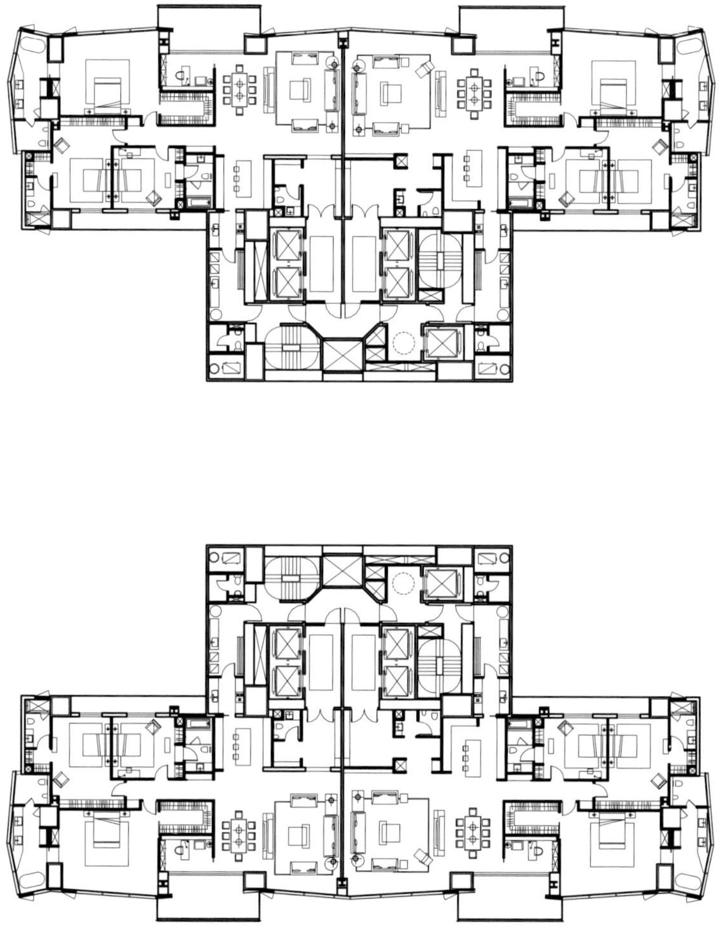

TYPICAL FLOOR PLAN

SOLITAIRE
TAICHUNG CITY, TAIWAN

MOTEL

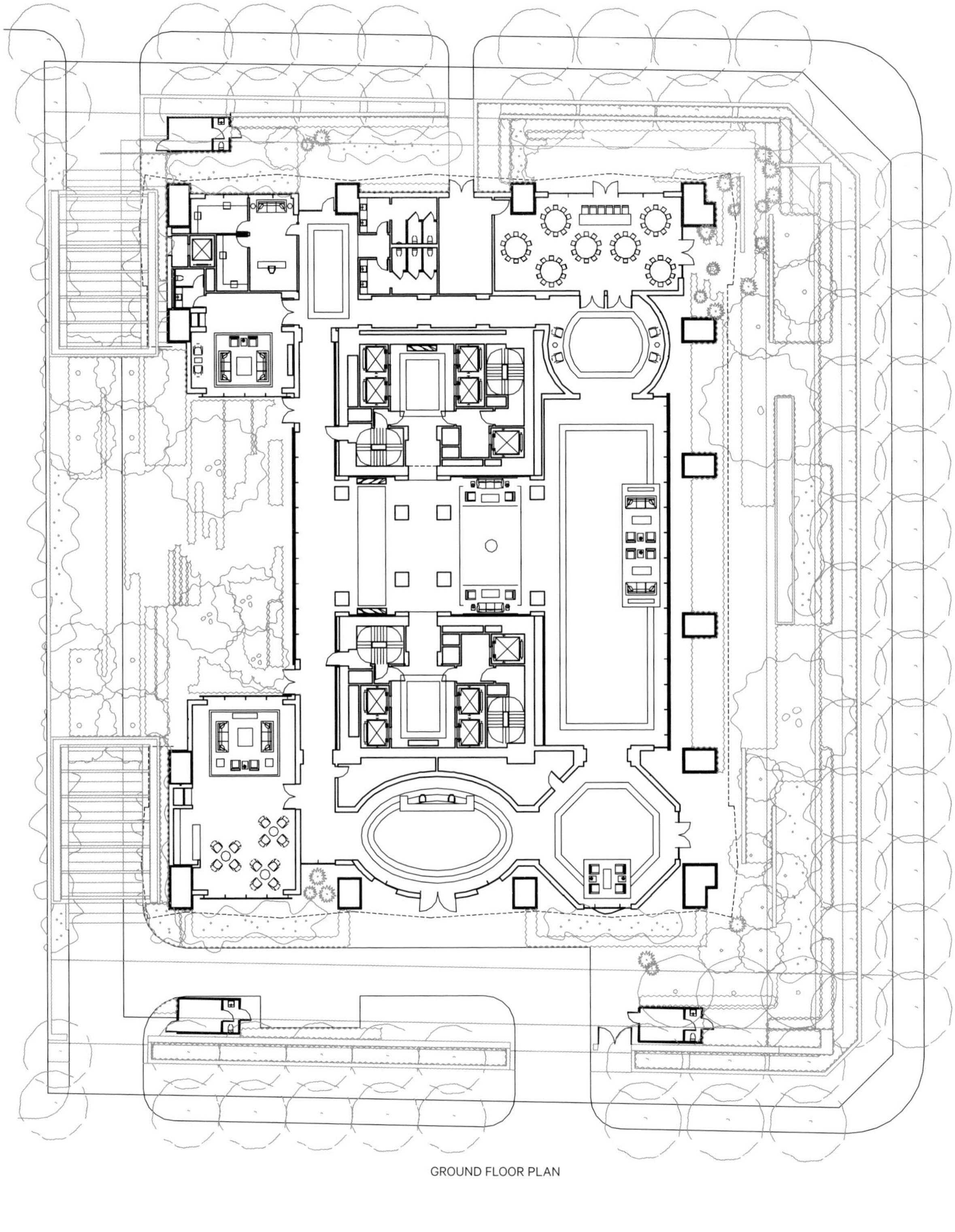

GROUND FLOOR PLAN

This 35-story residential tower in Taichung City is sited on a major boulevard in the central Seventh District. Designed with two luxury residences per floor ranging from 2,800 to 3,200 square feet, the building is configured to maximize views into the adjacent civic park and city center. A full range of amenities including a 25-meter indoor swimming pool, spa, gym, business center, tea rooms, and social lounge occupy the first and second floors. Valet motor court and social gardens complete the ground level.

SKY TOWER
TAICHUNG CITY, TAIWAN

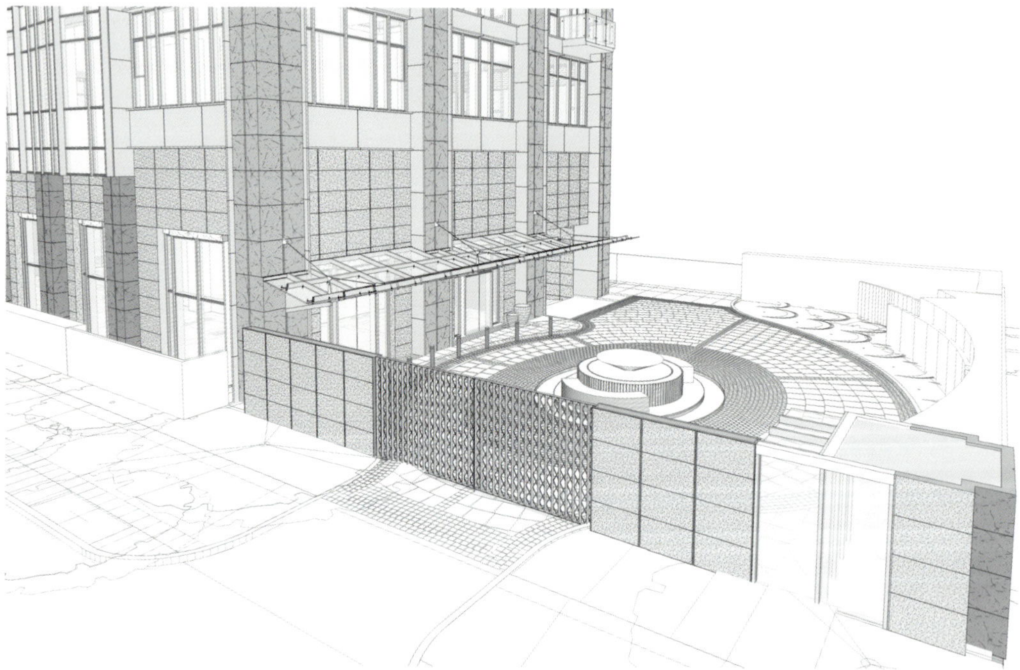

MOTORCOURT ENTRANCE

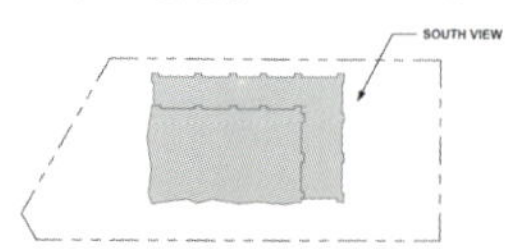

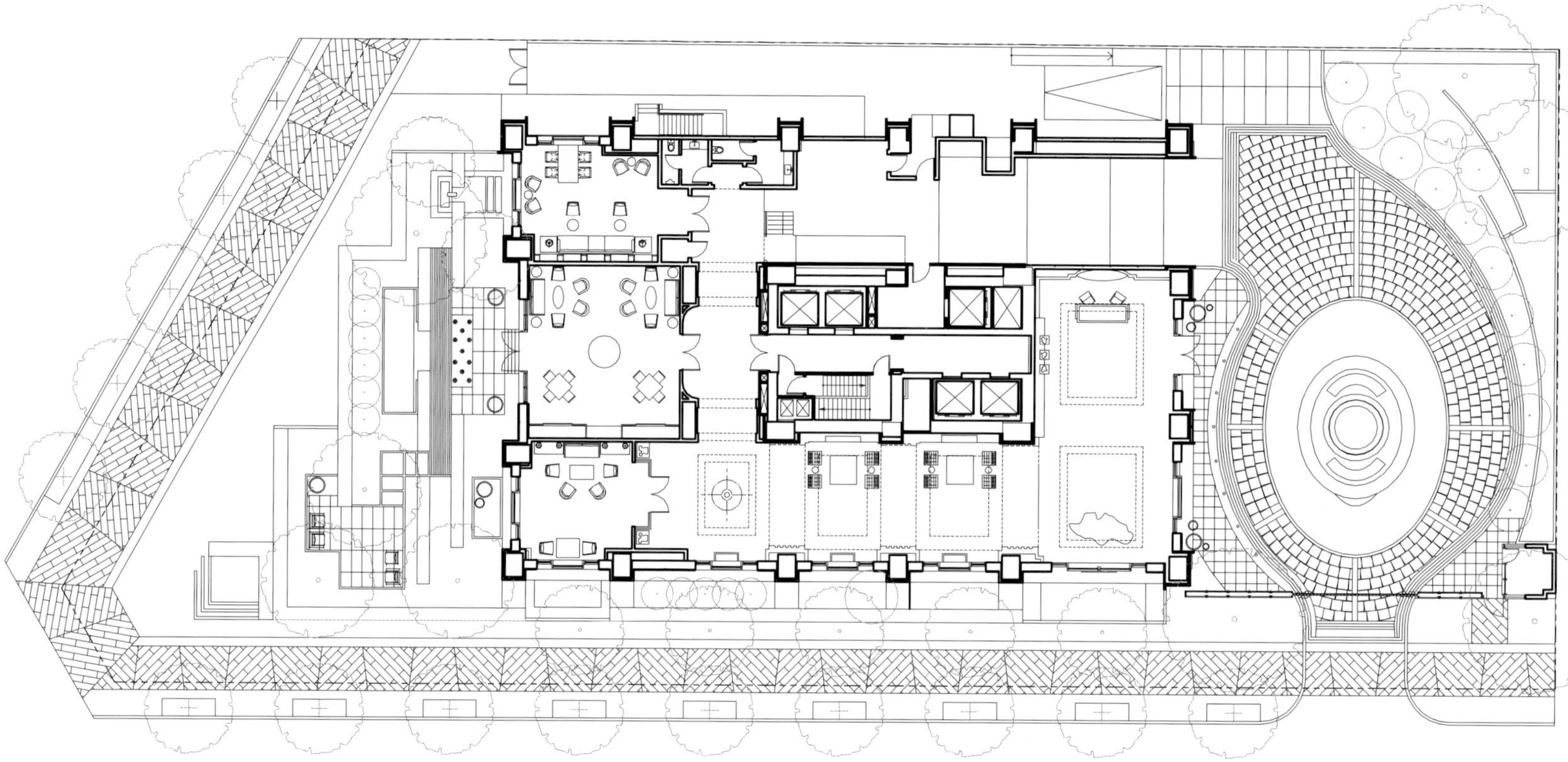

GROUND FLOOR PLAN

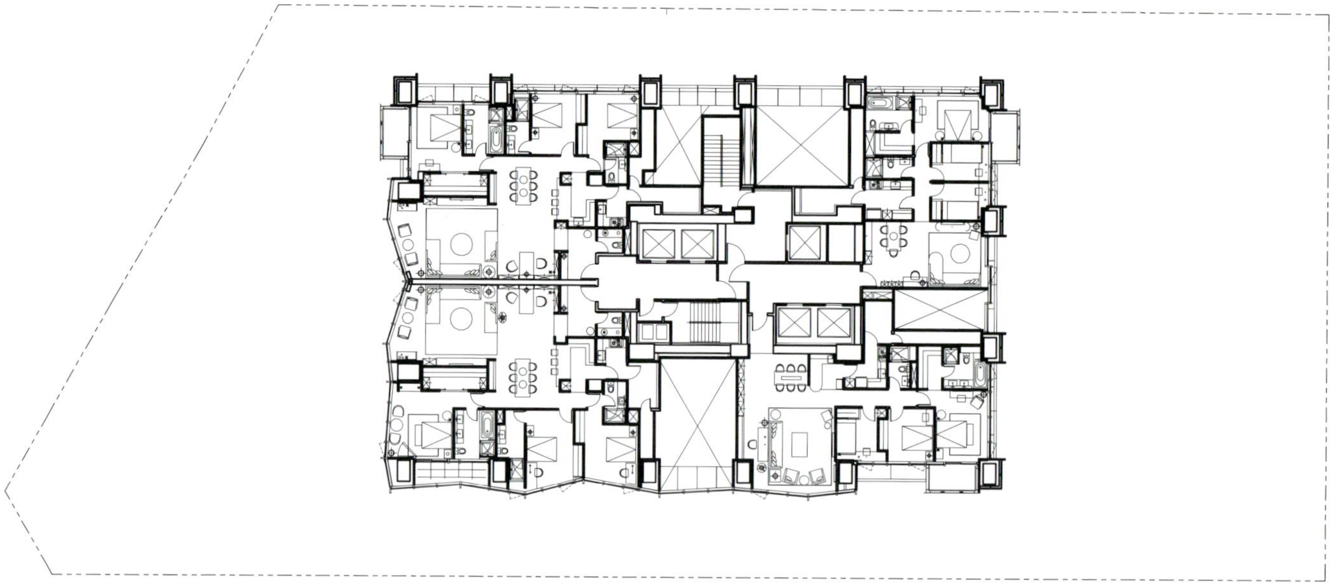

TYPICAL TOWER FLOOR PLAN

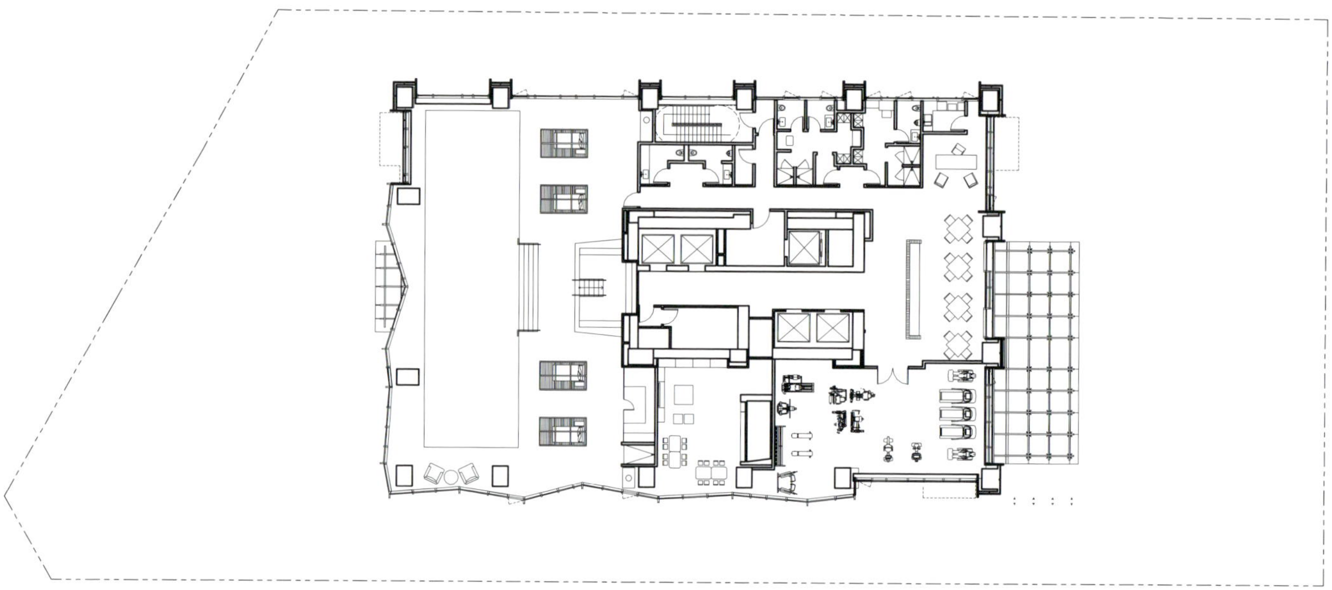

SECOND FLOOR AMENITY PLAN

This 26-story residential high-rise is located on the outskirts of Taichung's city center. Each floor is comprised of four residences, approximately 1,800 square feet in size. Due to its outlying location, the building has a full spectrum of amenities with gardens, swimming pool and spa, health club pavilion, social lounges, and business meeting rooms and support all on site. The roof deck is reserved for hospitality and food and beverage service and provides spectacular views to the city skyline.

CITY PARK
TAICHUNG CITY, TAIWAN

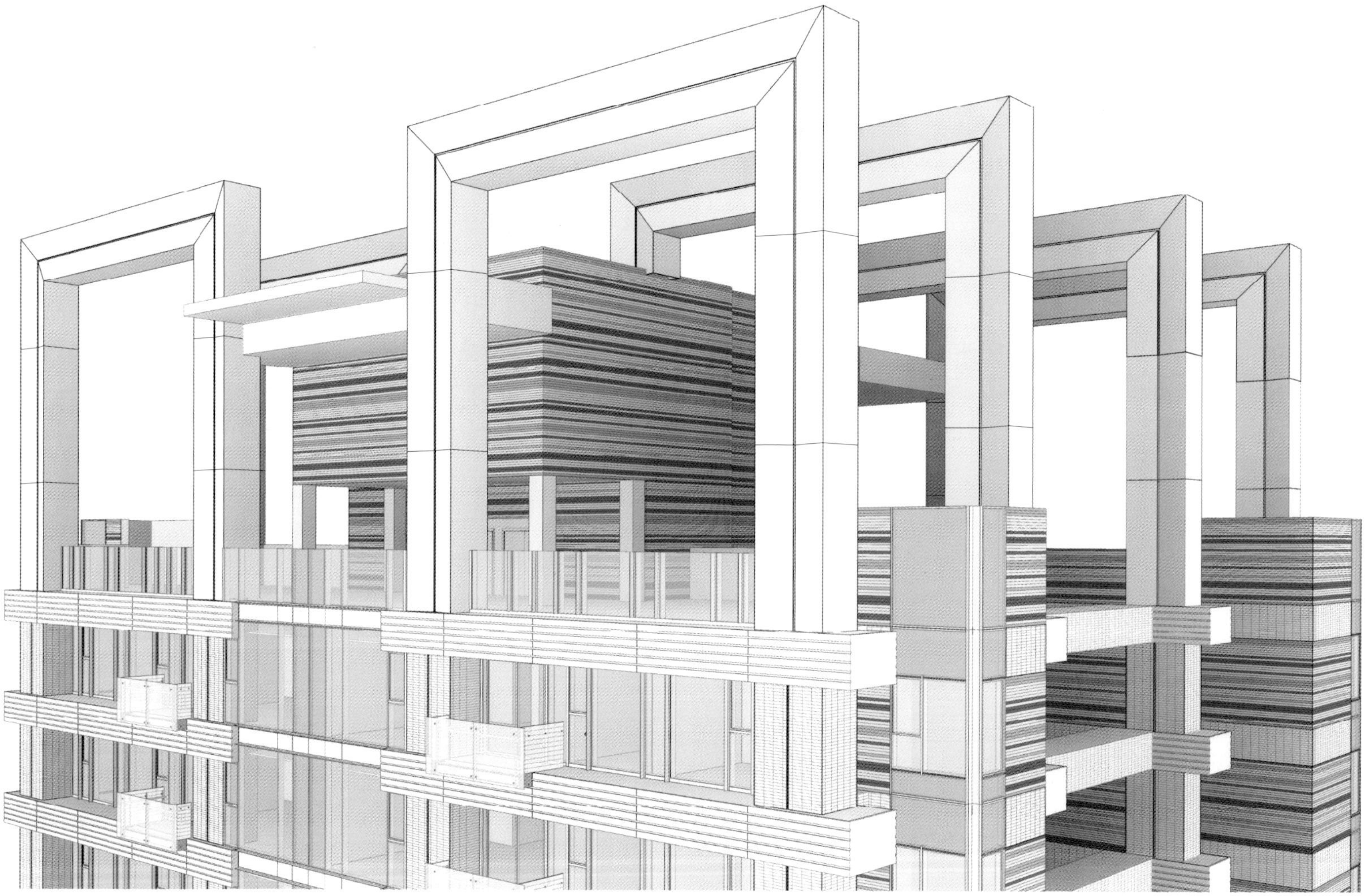

BUILDING TOP STUDY

AS52 RXZ

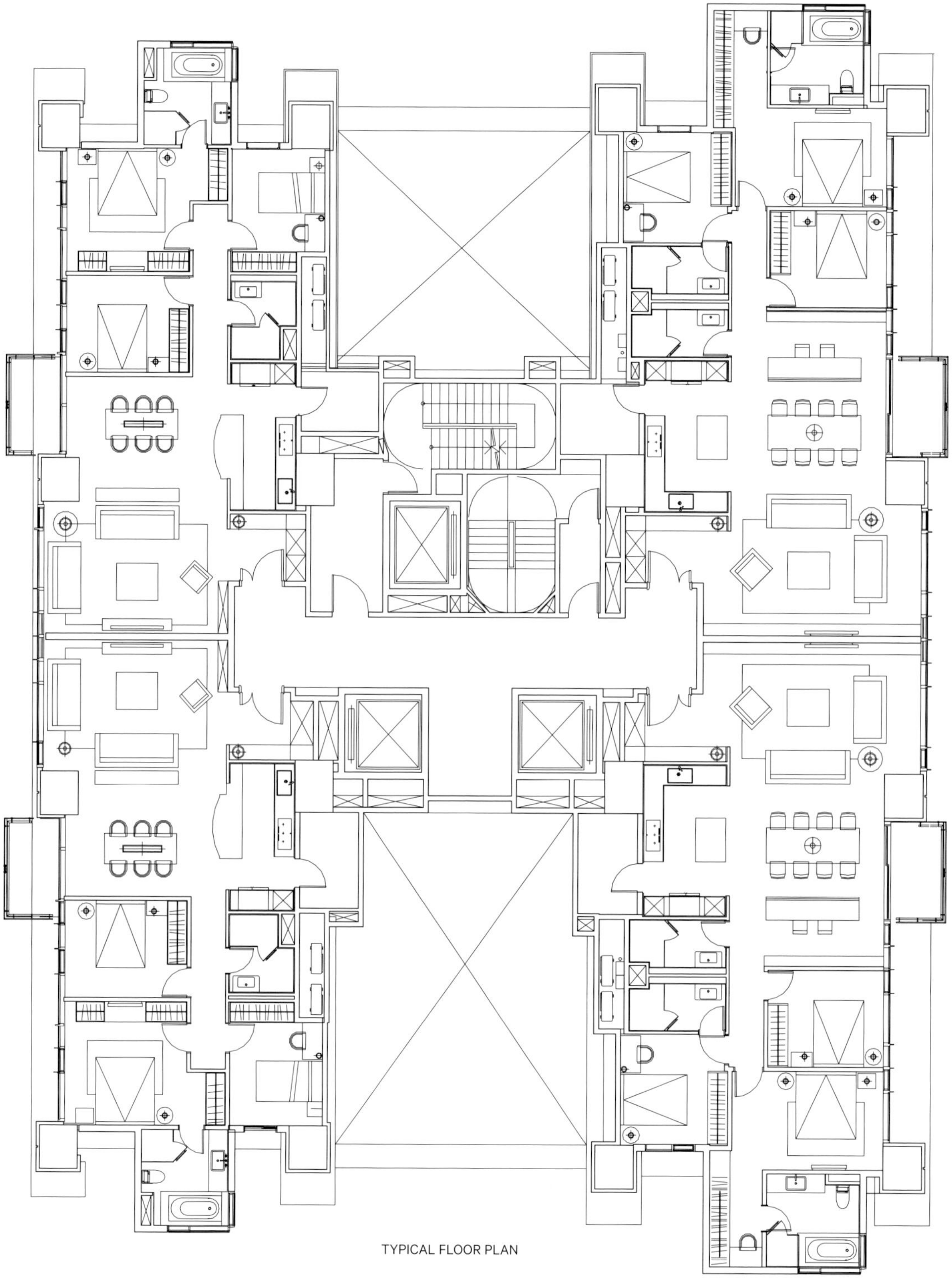

TYPICAL FLOOR PLAN

Located in an emerging urban neighborhood in Taichung City, this residential high-rise was designed for entry-level residents near to schools, shopping, and recreational public parks. Living, dining, and kitchen areas are open and shared while bedrooms and bathrooms are private. Secondary kitchens are provided for local food preparation as are housekeeping and service quarters. Residences range in size from 1,200 to 1,600 square feet and the exterior architecture expresses the tower's seismic concrete frame that supports the structure and allows for floor-to-ceiling windows maximizing views and sunlight.

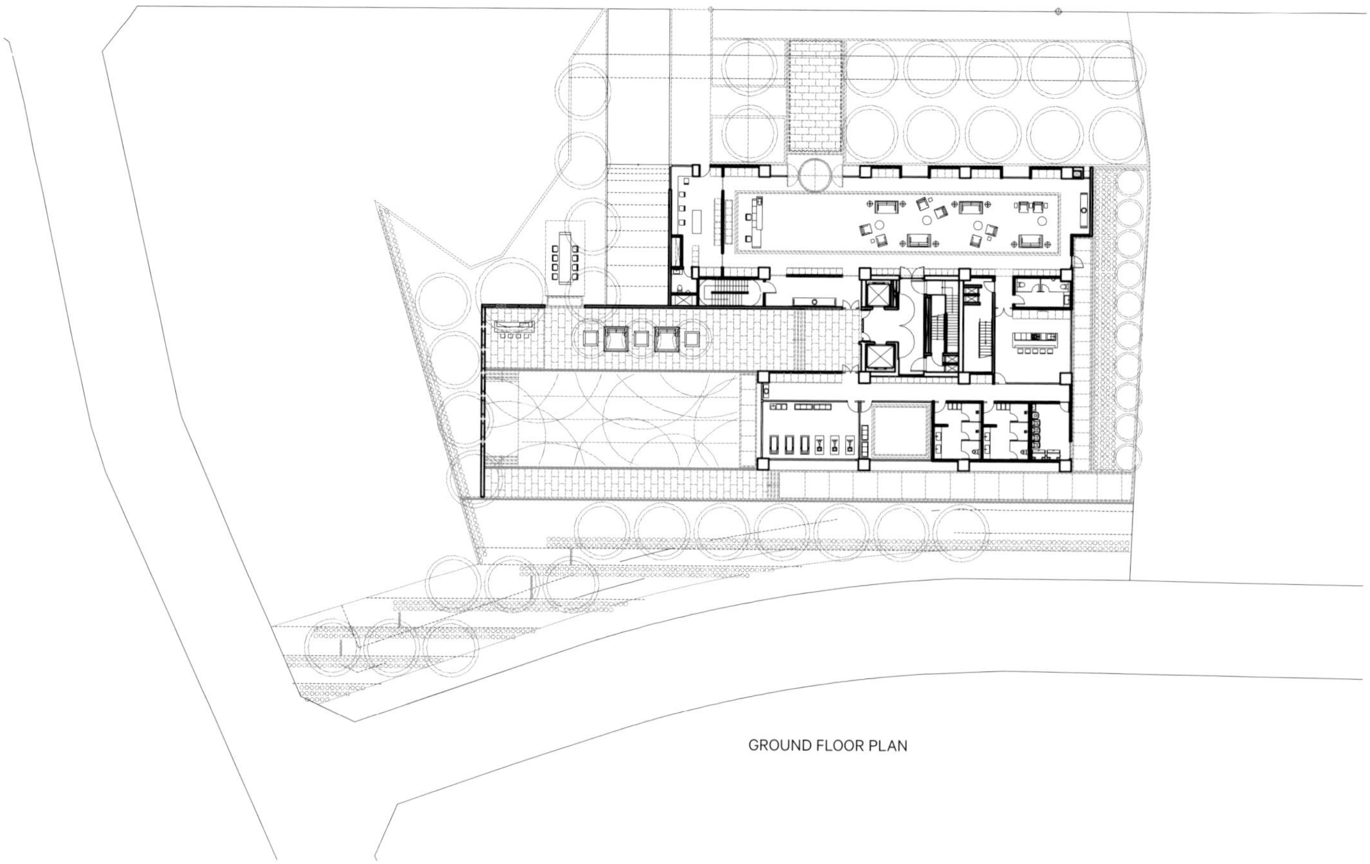

GROUND FLOOR PLAN

NANTUN
TAICHUNG CITY, TAIWAN

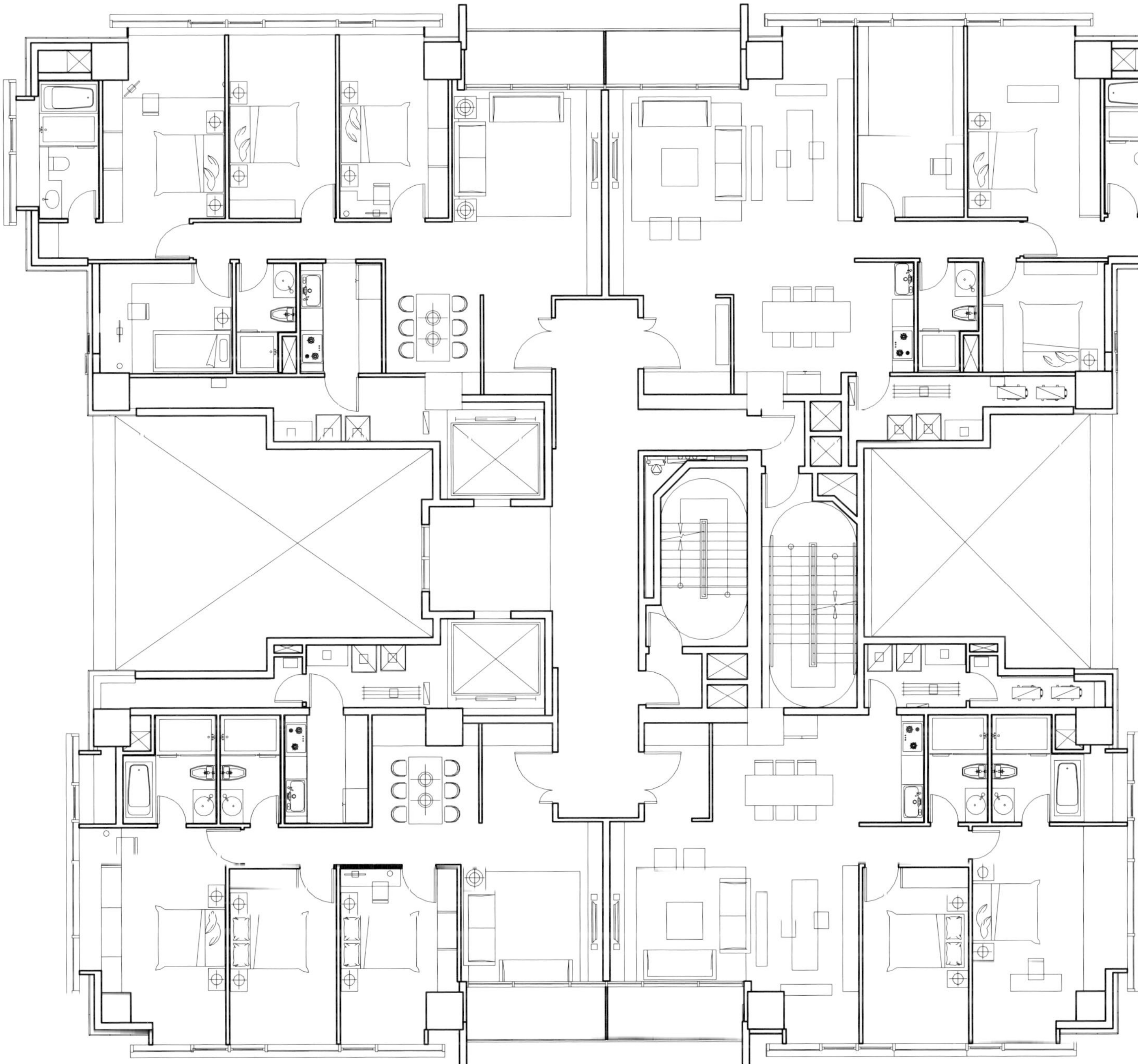

TYPICAL FLOOR PLAN

Located in the Golden Triangle of Jakarta, Indonesia's capital city, this premier twin tower residential complex is sited in a lush two-acre tropical garden setting. A single generous motor court unifies arrival to the project with one lobby for each tower and a wide range of social and recreational amenities on the ground floor. Direct and personalized vertical access is provided from the basement parking floors to the ground level and to residential floors that comprise a total of 300 residences. The buildings' exteriors are finished in natural stone and glass with broad balconies adjacent to living rooms. The roof is reserved for hospitality and social functions that enjoy skyline views.

VERDE II
JAKARTA, INDONESIA

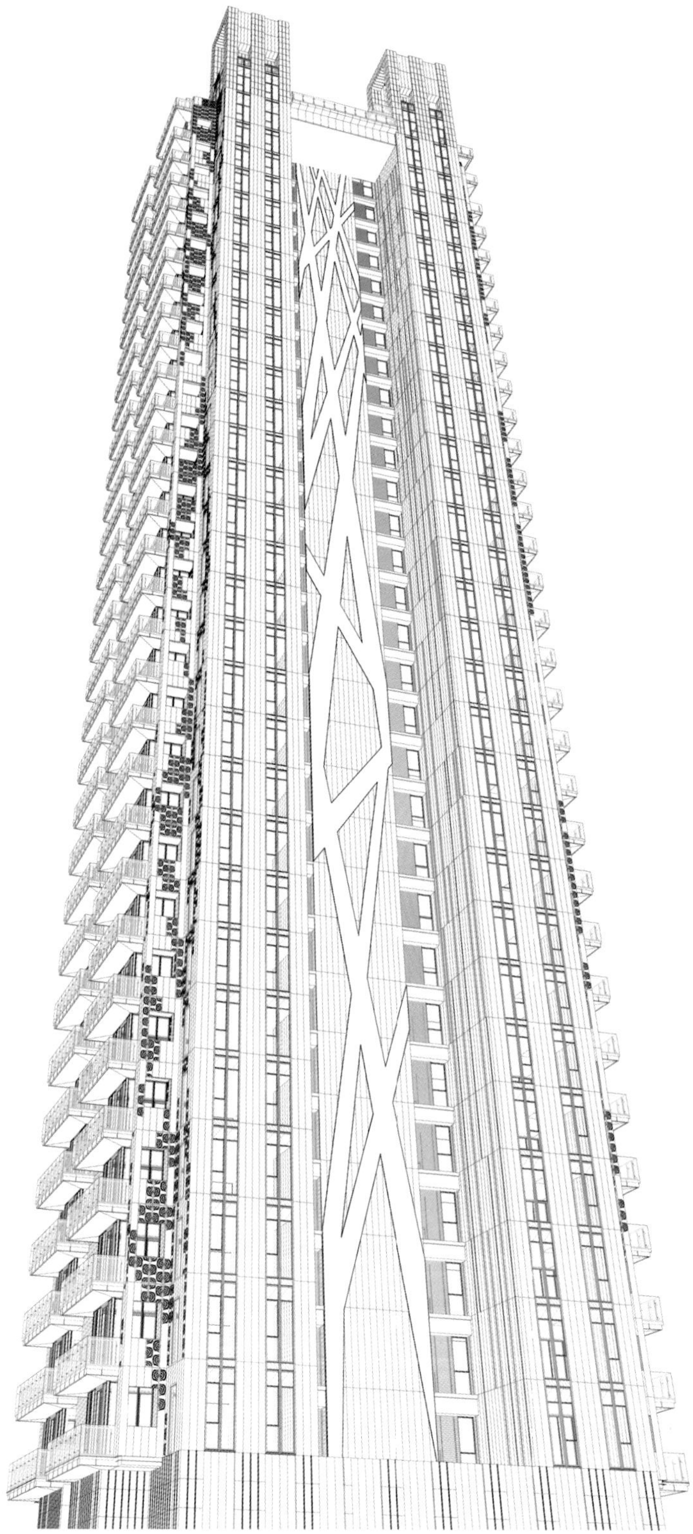

FACADE STUDY

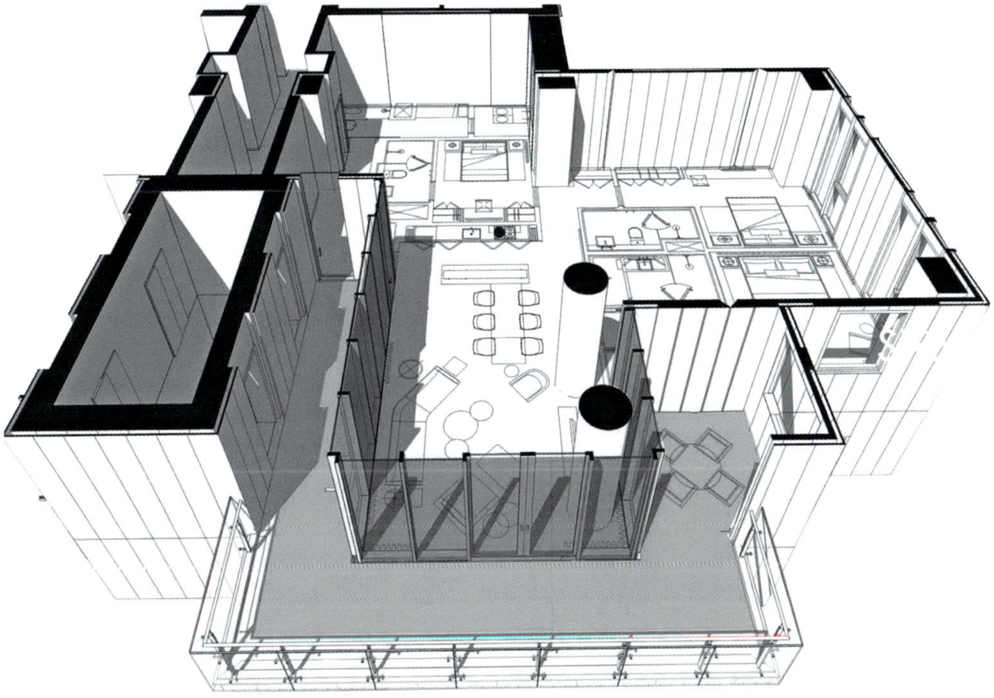

UNIT DIAGRAM-EXTERIOR TO INTERIOR

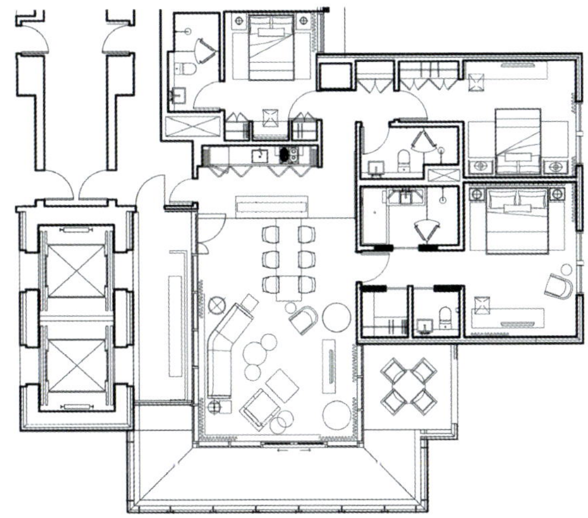

UNIT FLOOR PLAN

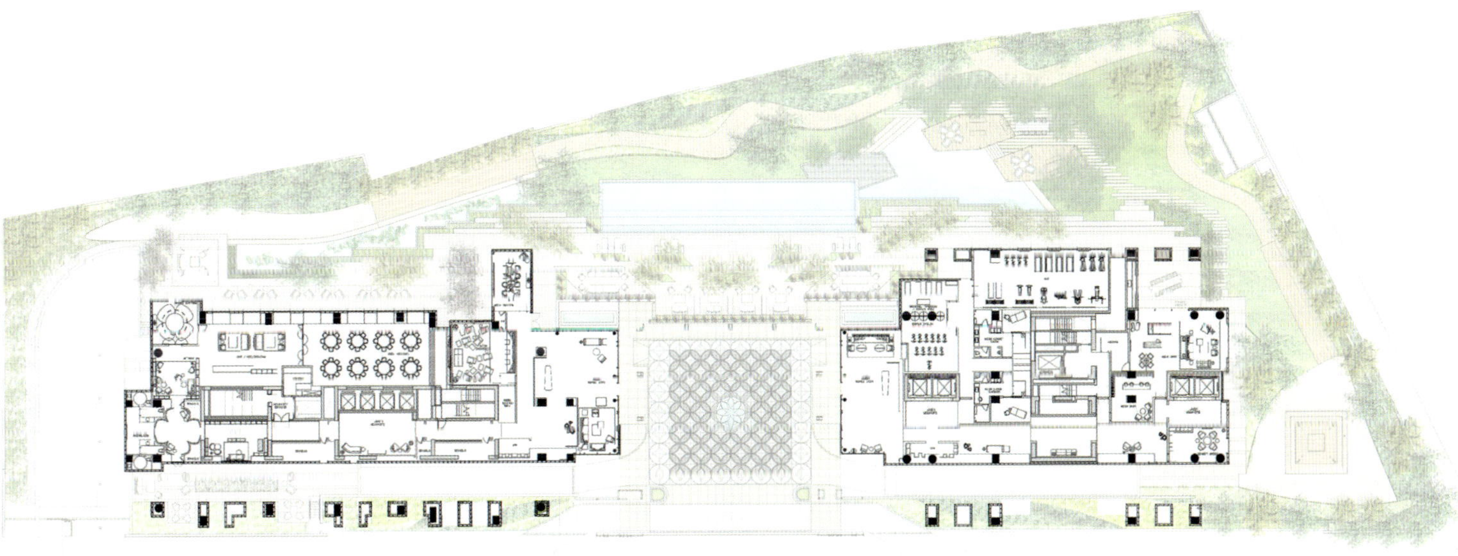

GROUND FLOOR PLAN

Figueroa Eight is a 41-story residential apartment tower in the heart of downtown Los Angeles. Located on a prominent one-acre site, this urban project includes over 400 apartments and 10,000 square feet of ground-floor commercial space. A generous residents amenity floor and terrace complete with swimming pool, spa, cabanas, indoor/outdoor social pavilion, gym, and outdoor culinary center sit atop three levels of above-grade parking. The rooftop encloses a resident's bar and social lounge, outdoor spa, and dining terrace. These amenities all enjoy a western view of the Santa Monica Mountains, the Pacific Ocean, and evening sunsets.

FIGUEROA EIGHT
LOS ANGELES, CALIFORNIA

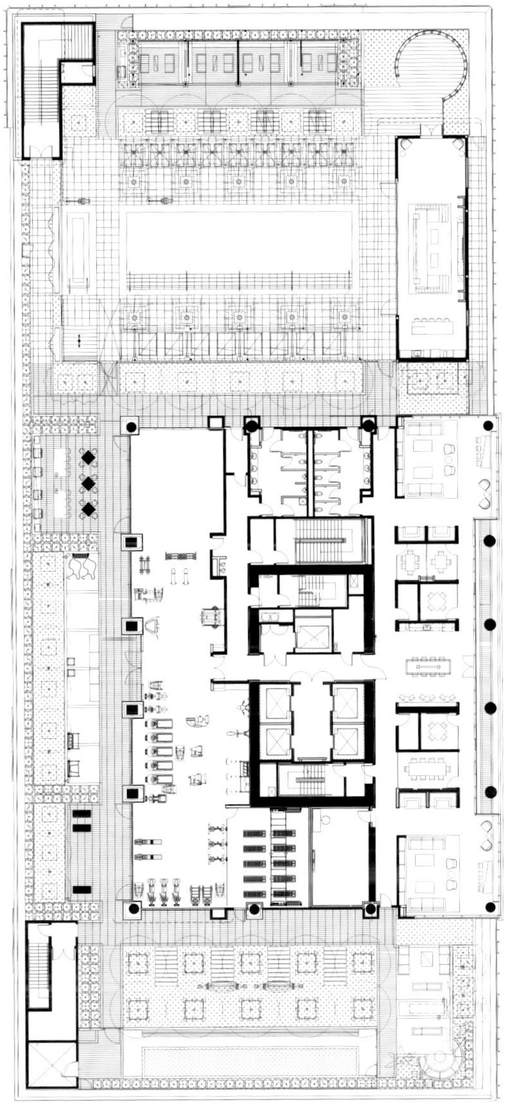
AMENITY DECK FLOOR PLAN

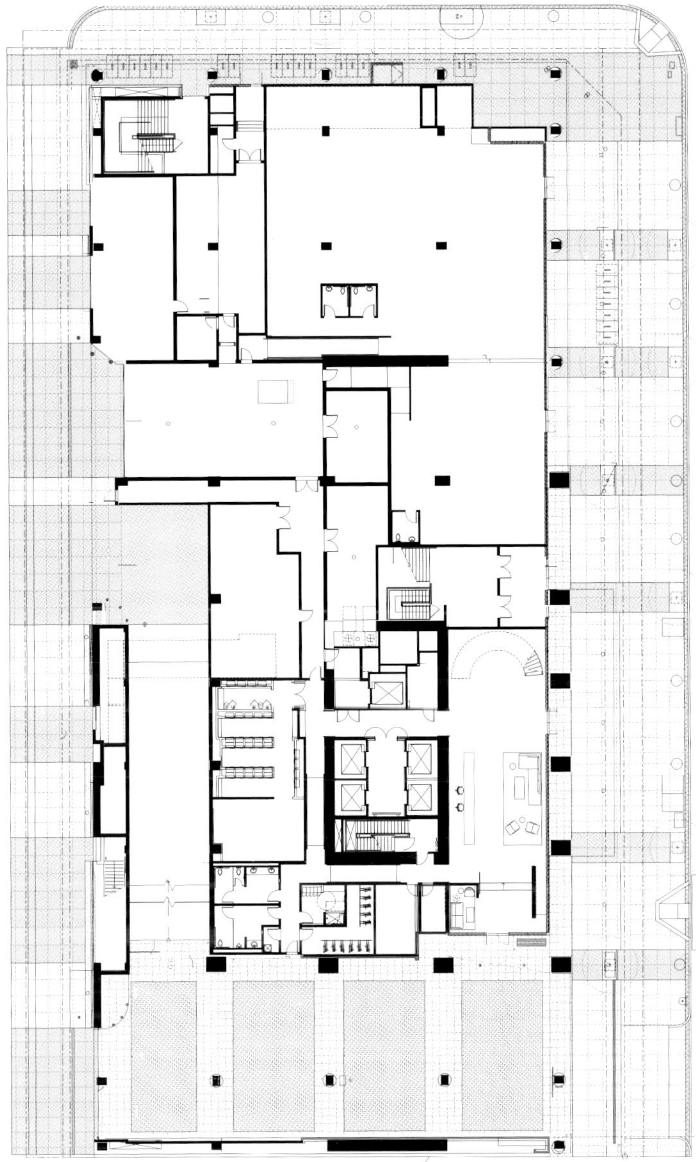
GROUND FLOOR PLAN

LOBBY STAIR

Coffe

Located in the heart of Hollywood at the corner of Sunset and Cahuenga Boulevards, 6400 Sunset is a 21-story residential tower with 200 residences above four levels of podium parking. Consistent with the City's Planning Department guidelines, the tower is sited on a north/south axis, preserving views between the hills and the Los Angeles basin, and providing all tower residents with sweeping views of the Hollywood Hills. All units enjoy floor-to-ceiling glass and operable windows to maximize sunlight, views, and air quality.

The rooftop of the podium serves as the recreational and social center of the project, including swimming pool, spa, large social and dining lounges, a dog park, grooming center, and garden-level residences. The tower roof houses penthouse apartments and additional amenities with 360-degree views of Los Angeles.

6400 SUNSET BOULEVARD

HOLLYWOOD, CALIFORNIA

CNN

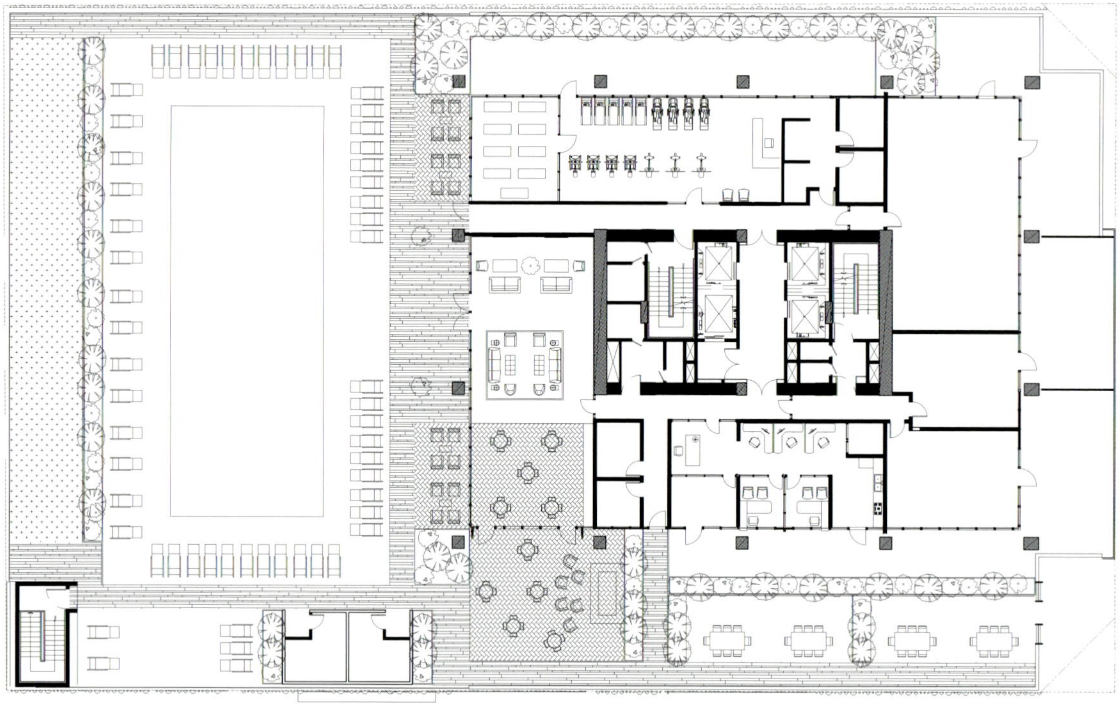

AMENITY DECK FLOOR PLAN

FACADE STUDY

Originally designed to house the offices of a legendary Hollywood film studio, Constellation Place is a 35-story Class A office tower comprising 700,000 square feet of contemporary workplace. To best suit the needs of its high-profile tenants, the floors are large, column-free with multiple glass corners on each floor to maximize sunlight and views. The dramatically curved exterior curtain wall encloses triangular glass corners highlighted by a richly detailed facade of various glass types and natural stones.

Sited on six acres at the corner of Constellation Boulevard and Century Park West, Constellation Place enjoys a highly visible and prominent position at the western edge of Century City. Retail, restaurants, entertainment, and hotels are a part of this vibrant mixed-use neighborhood. The project includes a six-story parking structure with the largest array of rooftop photovoltaic solar panels in the city of Los Angeles. Generous garden spaces have been designed around the perimeter of the tower to include native plantings, publicly accessible fine art, and a covered outdoor social/working lounge.

CONSTELLATION PLACE
CENTURY CITY, CALIFORNIA

MGM

14-23

TALL

CULTURE

COMMUNITY

CRAFT

HOME

Johnson Fain has worked with the Native American Cultural and Educational Authority of the State of Oklahoma since 1996 to master plan and design a Native American cultural center and museum, now called the First Americans Museum (FAM). The mission of the complex is the study, production, and celebration of all aspects of Native American culture on a 300-acre site on the Oklahoma River south of downtown Oklahoma City. The physical design grew out of Native American concepts of spirituality and the goal of achieving a seamless relationship between earth and building.

The architectural and landscape materials of the project draw from the three native ecologies: the woodlands, the river, and the plains. Monumental materials are employed such as earth, timber, natural stone, and Corten steel. Architectural space embraces the four primal elements—earth, fire, wind, and water—and the project is sited on a cardinal east/west axis to reference the diurnal journey of the sun in the sky. The Museum's massing reflects the intersection of two large circles, one representing Native residency, the other the Western European occupation. At the juncture lies the Hall of The People, a celebratory space surrounded by permanent and changing exhibitions, the FAMily Discovery Center, the social, culinary, and retail spaces collectively known as the Xchange and the FAM Theater.

FIRST AMERICANS MUSEUM
OKLAHOMA CITY, OKLAHOMA

ENTRANCE

SITE PLAN

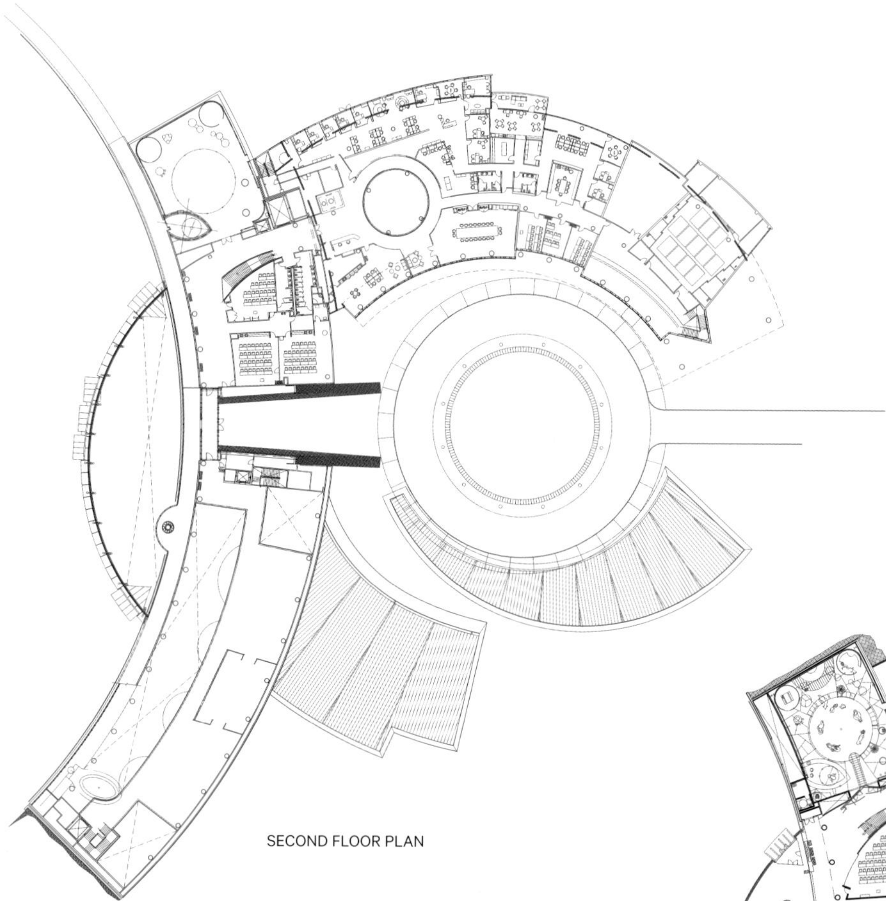

SECOND FLOOR PLAN

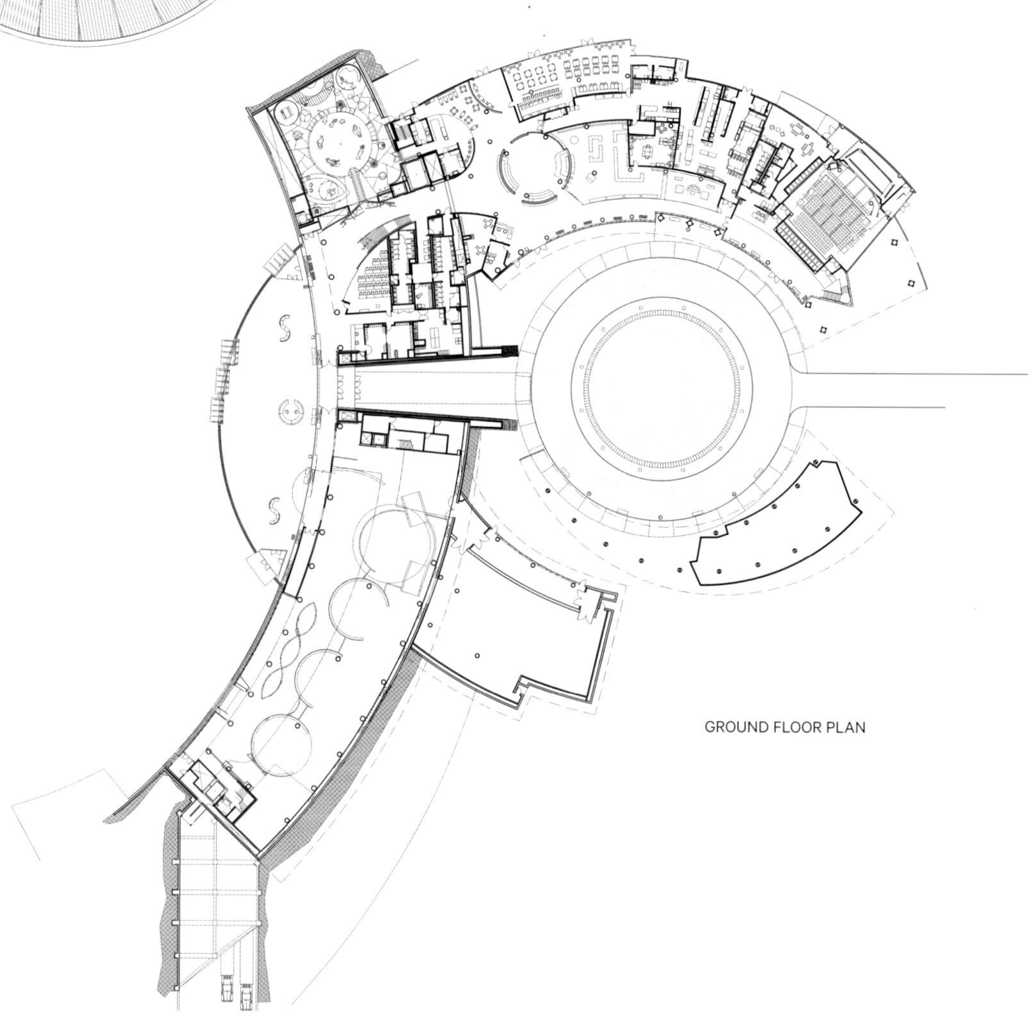

GROUND FLOOR PLAN

FAMstore

The Catholic Diocese of Orange acquired the Crystal Cathedral property in Garden Grove and retained Johnson Fain to substantially convert the Cathedral building to a place of Catholic worship to be named Christ Cathedral. The building, designed by Philip Johnson and John Burgee in the late 1970s, is sited as the centerpiece of a religious campus that also features the architecture of Richard Neutra and Richard Meier. A diamond-shaped plan elongated from east to west, the entrance to the cathedral is on the south at the Bishop's Door with the Predella, Altar, Ambo, and Cathedra located on axis against the north wall of the building. A custom-made platinum-leaf baldachin is suspended 30 feet above the altar in the 120-foot-tall volume of the building.

In an attempt to address an array of technical challenges and to employ architectural tools to heighten the sense of space and spirituality, 6,000 translucent, triangular "petals" were inserted into the structural space frame in various degrees of openness and closure. The acoustical diffusion of sound was improved, as was the ability to control glare and direct sunlight for greater comfort. In the darkness of evening, the petals allow reflected light to fill the sanctuary that makes the cathedral appear to glow from within. The new floors and low sanctuary walls are finished in white and gray natural stones to represent the earth, and the upper glass walls and ceilings, now translucent with faceted petals, represent the heavens.

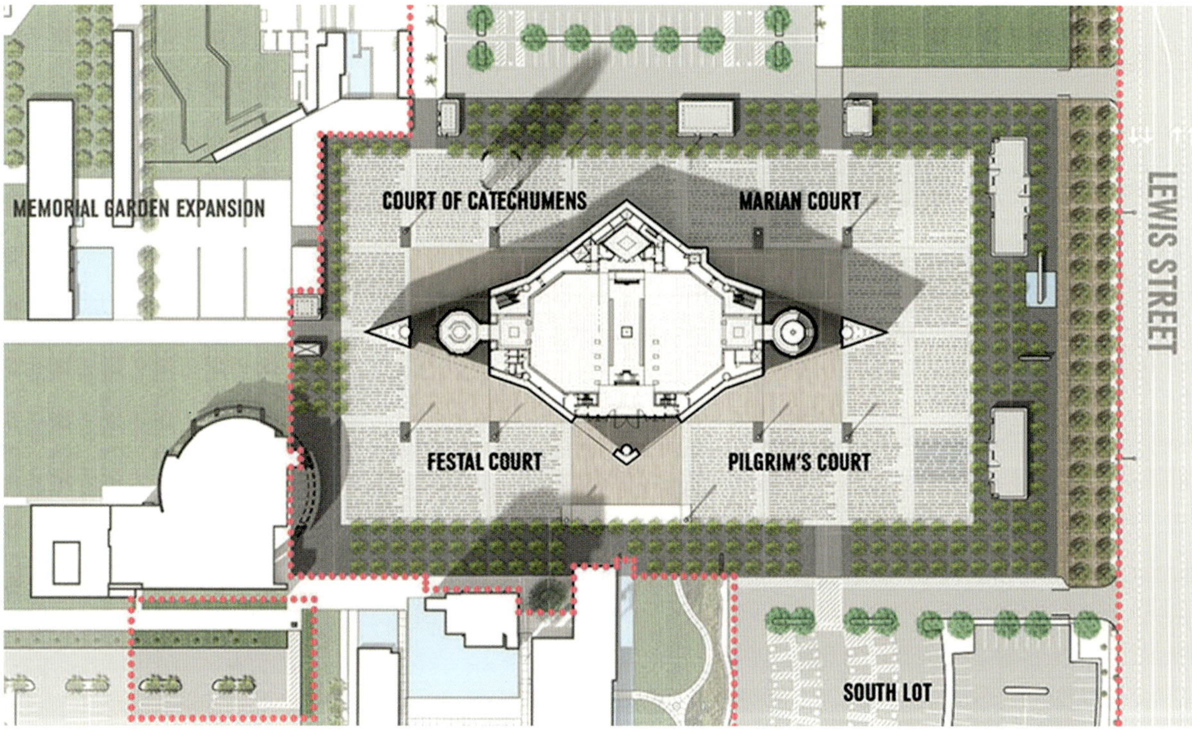

CHRIST CATHEDRAL
GARDEN GROVE, CALIFORNIA

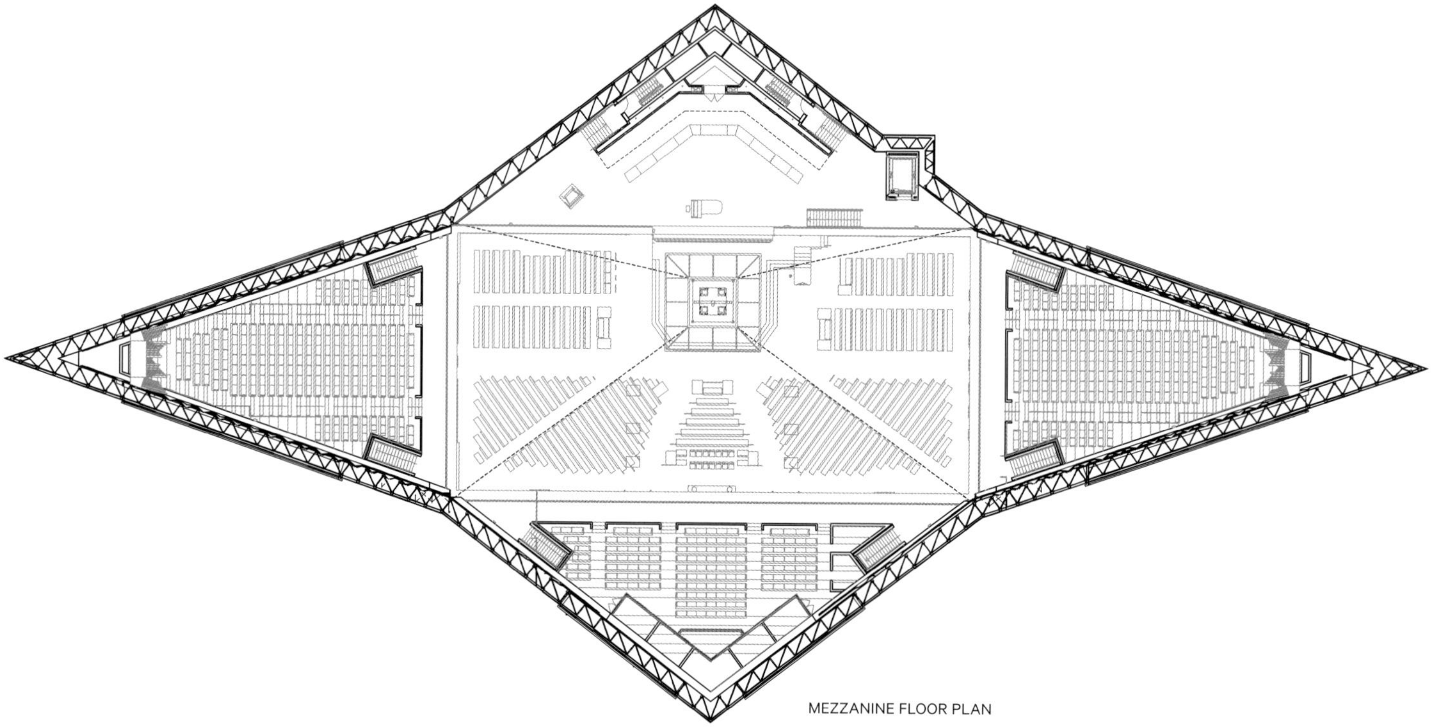

MEZZANINE FLOOR PLAN

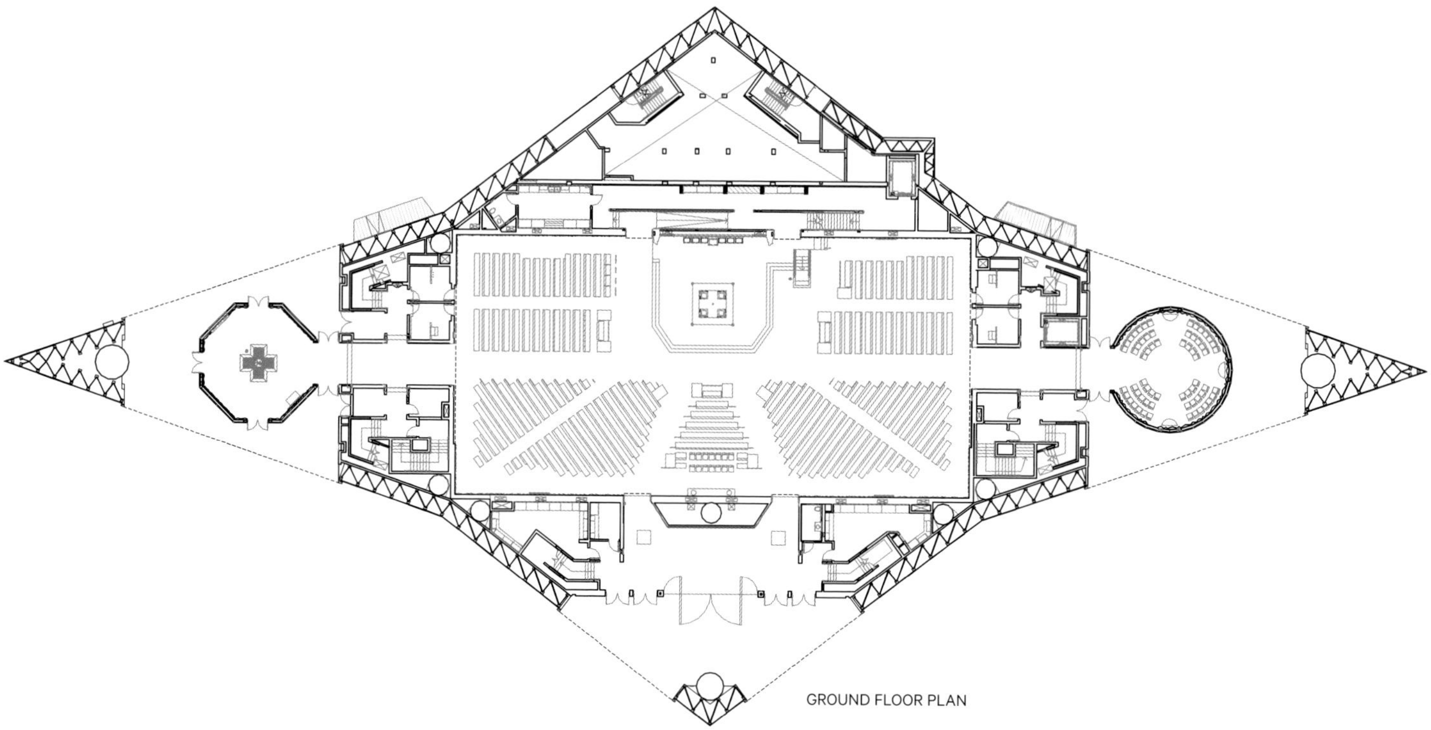

GROUND FLOOR PLAN

A PLEDGE OF THE GLORY TO COME + HOW HOLY THIS FEAST IN WHICH

OF THE SON, AND OF THE HOLY SPIRIT + GO, THEREFORE, AND MAKE DISCIPLES

Located at the easterly terminus of Capitol Park, this project is an ambitious multi-block mixed-use development that consolidated the headquarters operations of three major departments of California State government. The 6,400 employees of the Department of Health & Human Services, Education, and General Services are housed in the five-building, 1.5-million-square-foot complex along with 1,500 parking spaces.

The California Department of Education Headquarters, Block 225, was the first of this five-building development to be completed. Johnson Fain acted as the master design architect that included site planning and interior design. At 336,000 square feet and six stories, Block 225 was the largest project worldwide at the time to receive a LEED Gold certification after completion and has since been upgraded to LEED Platinum status. The Departments of Health & Human Services and General Services are housed in the second portion of the Capitol Area East End Complex and have received LEED Silver ratings.

Public amenities include retail, a community police station, a 300-seat auditorium, and a childcare center for up to 100 infants, toddlers, and preschoolers that includes an outdoor play area. Previously, employees were spread out over 20 properties throughout the region. The new complex has consolidated staff, reduced the need and reliance on rental space, increased employee productivity, and put 6,400 employees within walking distance of the central city, services, and major public transportation systems.

CAPITOL AREA EAST END COMPLEX
SACRAMENTO, CALIFORNIA

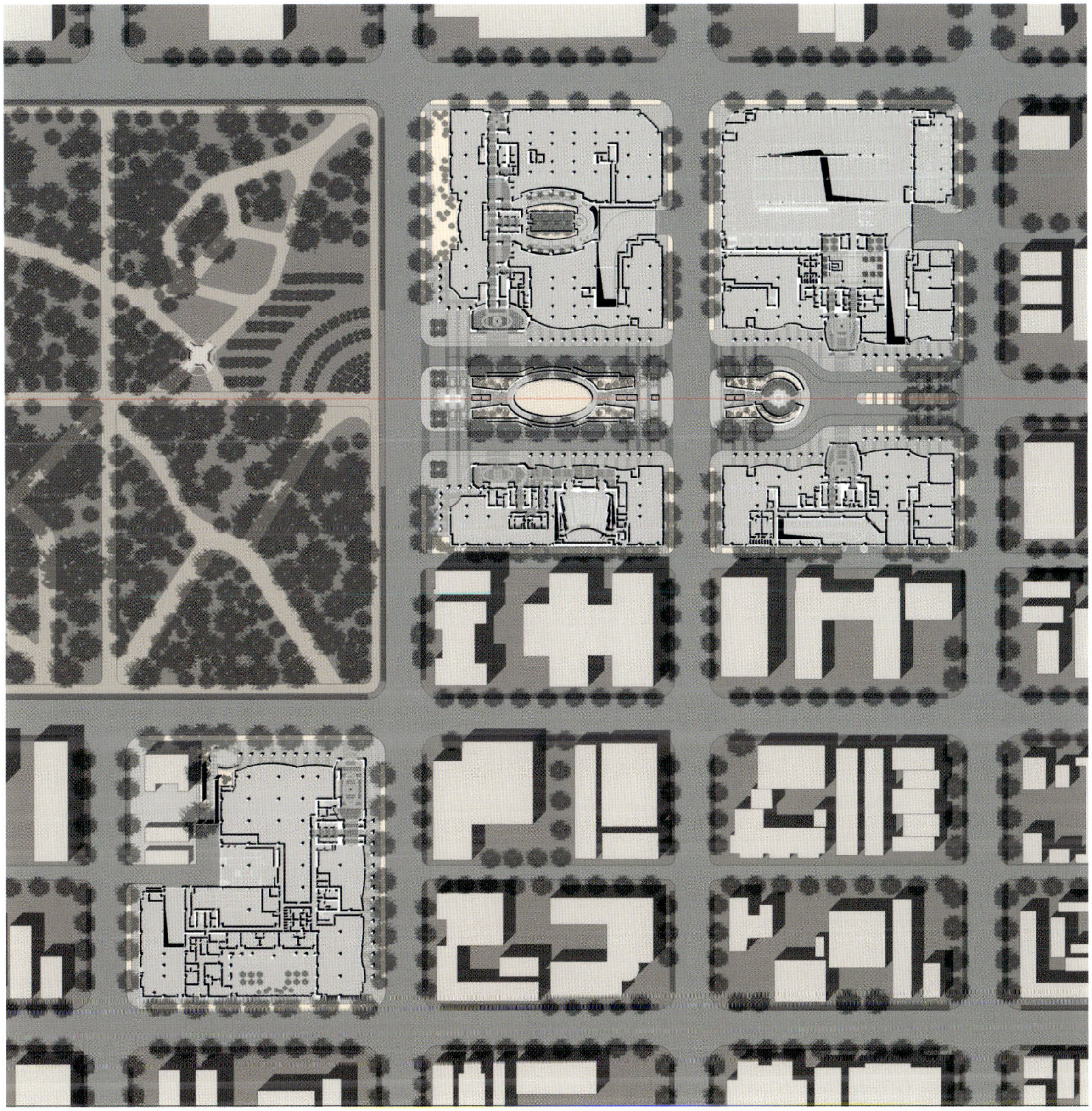

AREA PLAN

IT WAS THE SECRETS OF HEAVEN AND EARTH THAT I DESIRED TO LEARN.
MARY SHELLEY 1818
THE GREAT SEAL OF THE STATE OF CALIFORNIA
EUREKA

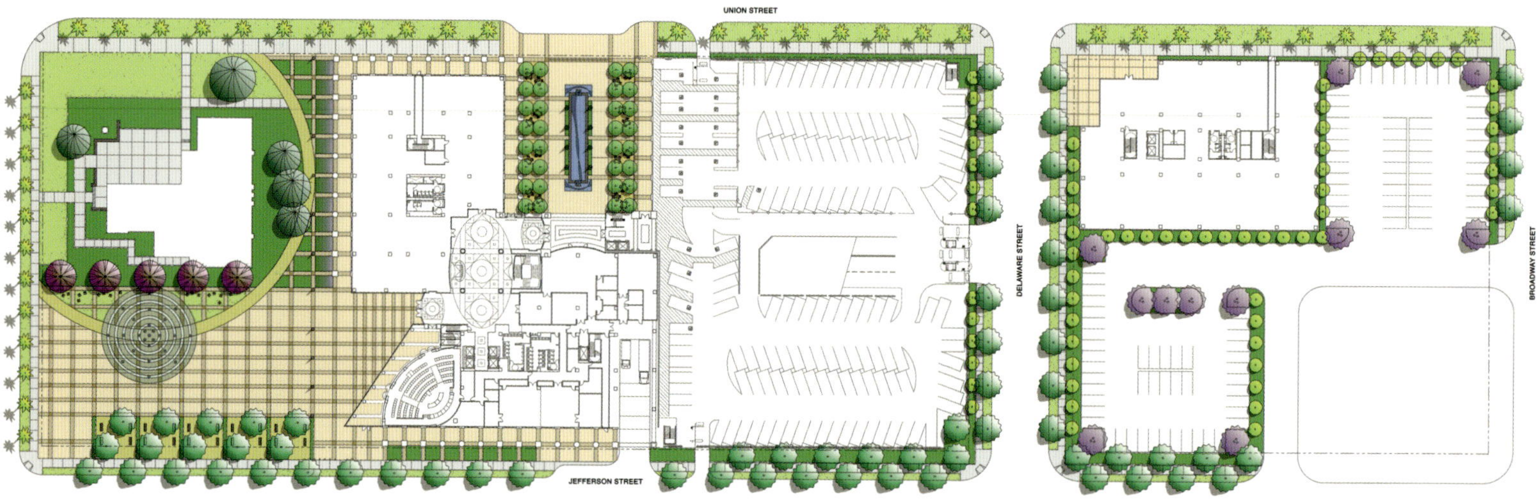

SITE PLAN

Solano County, one of the fastest growing counties in the State of California brought its many government departments together under one roof as part of a state-wide comprehensive consolidation effort. The project consists of a six-story, 300,000-square-foot administration building with a five-level parking garage equipped with a large photovoltaic array and multiple electric vehicle stations, plus an adjacent two-story, 43,000-square-foot probation building and a 25,000-square-foot public plaza. The new Government Center now houses over 800 county employees, combining 16 departments from 15 different locations in two cities. The project embodies the smart-growth strategies of modern infill development located within walking distance of Main Street and a multi-modal transportation center.

The six-story administration building, LEED Silver certified, incorporates many sustainable features including building materials with recycled content and a gray-water recovery system. The building also exceeds California's Title 24 Energy Efficiency Standards using high-efficiency electrical equipment, low ambient lighting systems, and a large photovoltaic array. The principal project goal was to create a landmark community building at the historic center of Fairfield. The generous central lobby incorporates publicly funded artwork and serves as a public gathering space for exhibits, press conferences, and community events.

SOLANO COUNTY GOVERNMENT CENTER
FAIRFIELD, CALIFORNIA

This new research laboratory and workplace complex for BioMarin will be located in the historic city of San Rafael, north of San Francisco. The new development, just one block from the downtown core, represents a new direction in growth for the existing campus. The full city block site contains a five-story senior housing center with apartments. A large open plaza fronts the complex at the building entry with a unique outdoor space under a cantilevered portion of the building that is the “front porch” and cafe for staff. The building’s shape, orientation, and shading all help to create a highly sustainable project. A large, landscaped roof deck between the two buildings offers a creative work environment for this innovative biotechnology company.

BIOMARIN
SAN RAPHAEL, CALIFORNIA

BIOMARIN
BIOMARIN

GROUND FLOOR PLAN

SECOND FLOOR PLAN

BIOMARIN
BIOMARIN

FOOD
CAFE COFFEE PASTRY SNACKS

Genentech, headquartered in South San Francisco, is a world leader in biotechnology. Johnson Fain has provided a wide range of design services for Genentech including master planning, architecture, and interior design. At the heart of its campus is a new administrative office complex. This multi-phase project, the result of a design-build process, is located on a bluff overlooking the San Francisco Bay and consists of three five-story office buildings clustered around a circular courtyard. Ground floors contain common facilities for the employees including a cafeteria, Genentech Store, and conference and meeting rooms.

The exterior treatment of the building facades reflects the interior functions of the activities within, and are composed of natural, sustainable, and durable materials. Private offices on the upper floors take advantage of the extraordinary outward views of the San Francisco Bay while common space and conferencing look to the landscaped courtyard within the site.

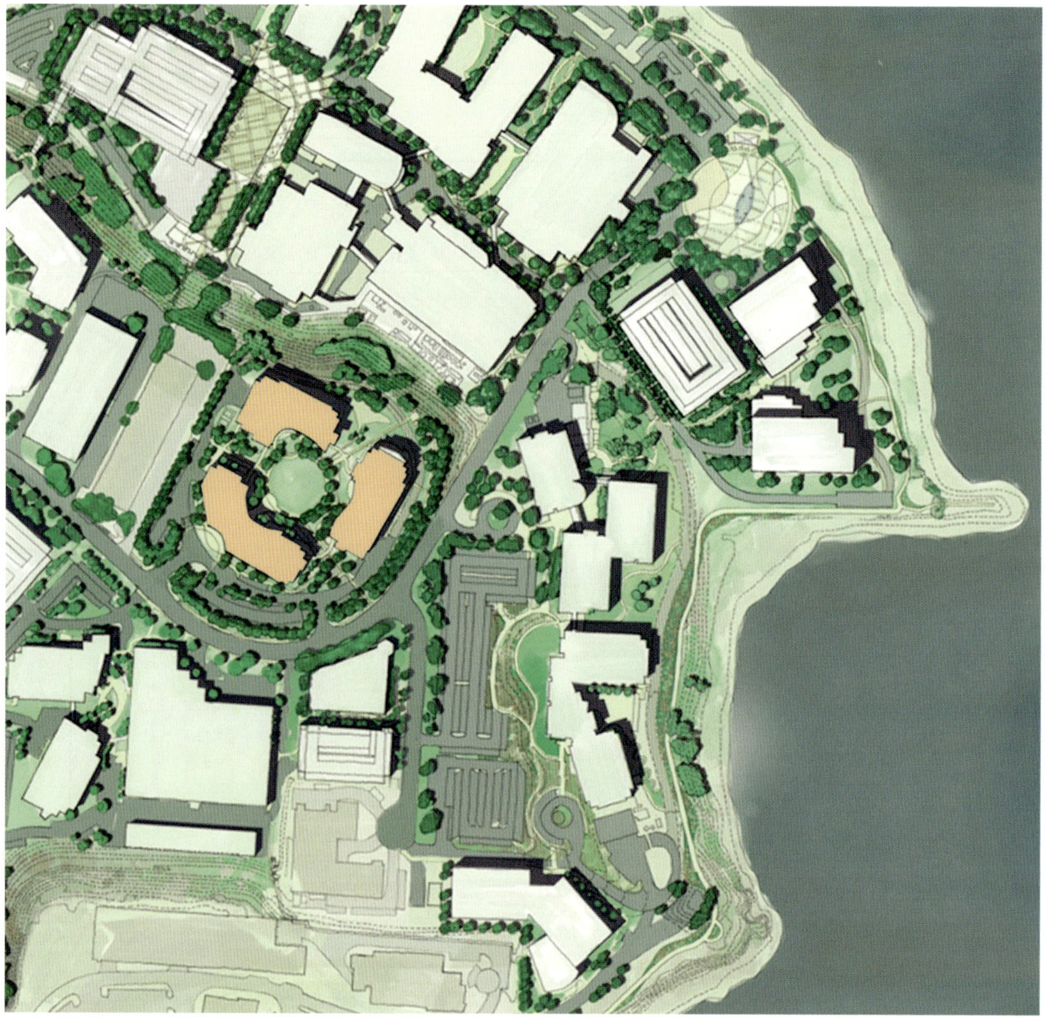

SITE PLAN

GENENTECH HEADQUARTERS
SOUTH SAN FRANCISCO, CALIFORNIA

1531

1531

Amgen, Inc. is one of the largest biotechnology companies in the world. Johnson Fain has provided comprehensive design services at Amgen Center since 1994. Three decades ago, Amgen began as a corporate start-up in a single building in Thousand Oaks. As the company grew, it acquired adjoining properties as they became available until the present 130-acre site was fully assembled. A master plan concept was established to accommodate expansion of new buildings, the adaptive reuse of existing buildings, and to reconfigure open spaces for improved pedestrian and automobile circulation and new employee services. These many projects have had the effect of transforming a formerly industrial neighborhood into a friendly, landscaped, and highly amenitized environment.

MASTER PLAN

AMGEN CENTER
THOUSAND OAKS, CALIFORNIA

This new research facility on the University of California, Berkeley campus is one of many projects initiated by the California State Center for Information Technology Research in the Interest of Society (CITRIS) and was planned to fuel economic growth through technology research and manufacturing. Designed to turn research into socially useful commercial applications, the facility includes classroom and laboratories plus a 149-seat auditorium, cybercafe, technology museum, and distance-learning classrooms. The Marvell Nanofabrication Laboratory is comprised of two large cleanrooms equipped with some of the world's most advanced semiconductor-fabrication equipment.

Named Sutardja Dai Hall, it is now the new home of CITRIS and the Banatao Institute @ Citris Berkeley. CITRIS is a multi-disciplinary program that combines the skills of more than 300 faculty researchers and thousands of students from four UC campuses—Berkeley, Davis, Merced, and Santa Cruz—with industrial partners from more than 60 corporations. As the headquarters for CITRIS, the 141,000 square-foot building is open to researchers from the four UC campuses in wide-ranging disciplines, including engineering, energy, health, law, public policy, political science, and new media. The new building replaces Davis Hall North in the northeast corner of the UC Berkeley campus and within the College of Engineering Quadrant. The design, massing, and scale of the five-story building is intended to respond to the nearby Arts & Crafts building as well as the adjacent Naval Architecture Building.

GROUND FLOOR PLAN

SUTARDJA DAI HALL
UNIVERSITY OF CALIFORNIA, BERKELEY

SUTARDJA DAI HALL

SUTARDJA DAI HALL

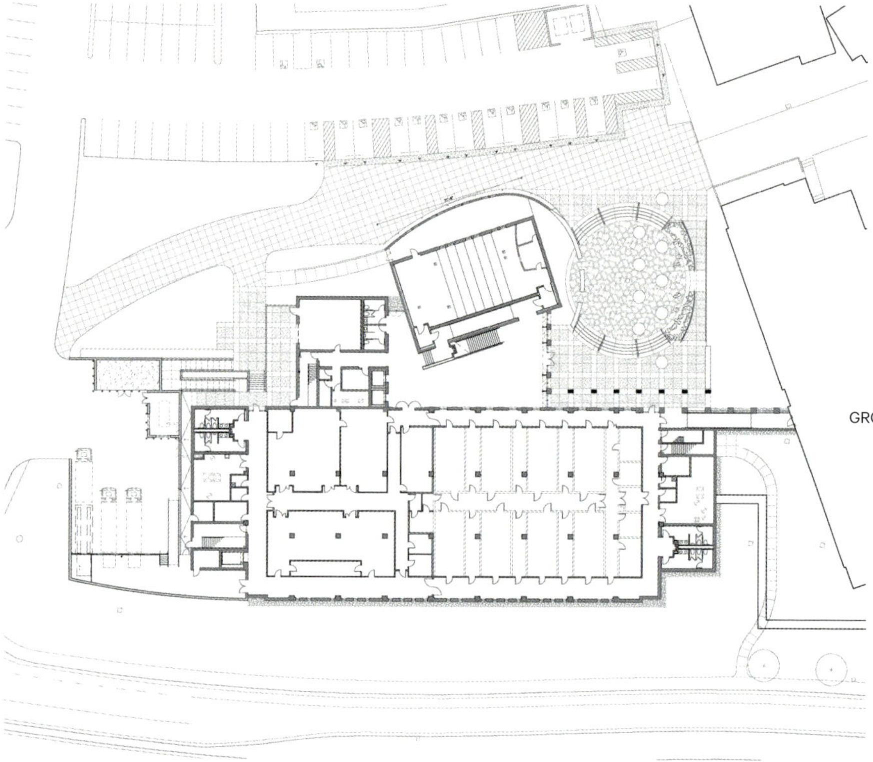

GROUND FLOOR PLAN

The California Institute for Telecommunications and Information Technology (Cal IT^2) is a new high-technology research and development facility at the University of California at Irvine. The project is one of the California State Institutes for Science and Innovation that was initiated and funded by the Governor's Office. The new building provides a physical platform for a wide range of multidisciplinary projects and programs for the School of Engineering, the Office of Academic Computing, Environmental Science, Media Arts, and the School of Education. Cal IT^2 supports these programs' research in information technology and innovative uses of digital media.

Encompassing 120,000 square feet of research and academic space in four stories, the building includes a combination of clean rooms for silicon chip-based manufacturing processes, wet and dry laboratories, classrooms, offices, and meeting facilities. Included are rooms for experimental media and a gallery for the display and demonstration of experiments in new media and technology. The building is composed of two major wings, one for research, manufacturing, and classrooms and the other for a 100-seat multi-media lecture, media center, and offices.

CAL IT^2
UNIVERSITY OF CALIFORNIA, IRVINE

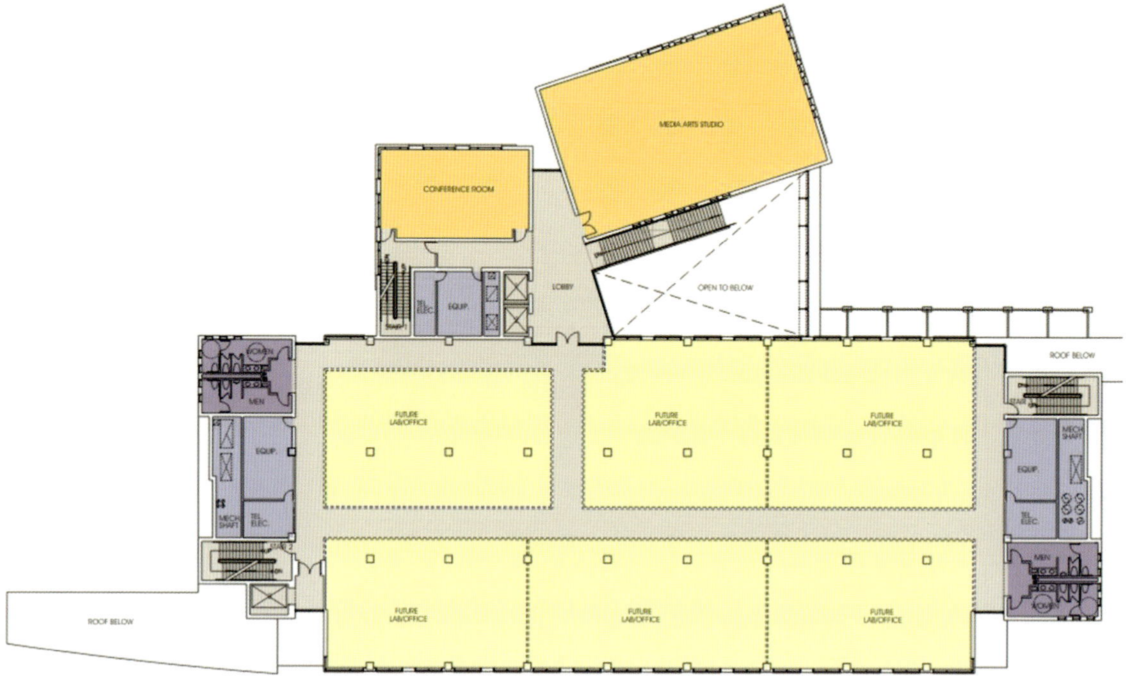

SECOND FLOOR PLAN

GROUND FLOOR PLAN

CALIFORNIA INSTITUTE
FOR TELECOMMUNICATION
AND INFORMATION TECHNOLO
Innovate.
Integrate.
Ignite.

STOP AHEAD
STOP

EDAX

One of the largest high schools in the Los Angeles Unified School District, Miguel Contreras Learning Center is located on 18 acres in the Crown Hill District of downtown Los Angeles. The project addresses critical overcrowding at nearby schools by providing 71 classrooms and major athletic facilities shared with other schools in the district. Facilities that can be shared with the community at large, such as the auditorium, are located at one end of the site to avoid disruption to classes at the other end. Reflecting the density and scale of its urban location, the high school accommodates approximately 1,700 students in 220,000 square feet of space and is comprised of an auditorium/administration building, two classroom wings, library/multi-media labs, and food services center.

The classroom wings are distinctive with their open-air corridors and stairs and floating corrugated steel roofs located to provide protection from the inclement weather and promote natural ventilation. The courtyard is designed as an extension of ground-level teaching rooms. These include an outdoor music garden adjacent to the Instrumental Music classroom, an outdoor stage platform adjacent to the Dance classroom, herb garden and informal “cook out” pergola adjacent to the Culinary Arts classroom, and a stepped gallery for outdoor artworks exhibition. The two gymnasia, sports fields, an Olympic-size swimming pool and parking structure are located in the northern portion of the site reachable by a pedestrian bridge.

MIGUEL CONTRERAS LEARNING CENTER
LOS ANGELES, CALIFORNIA

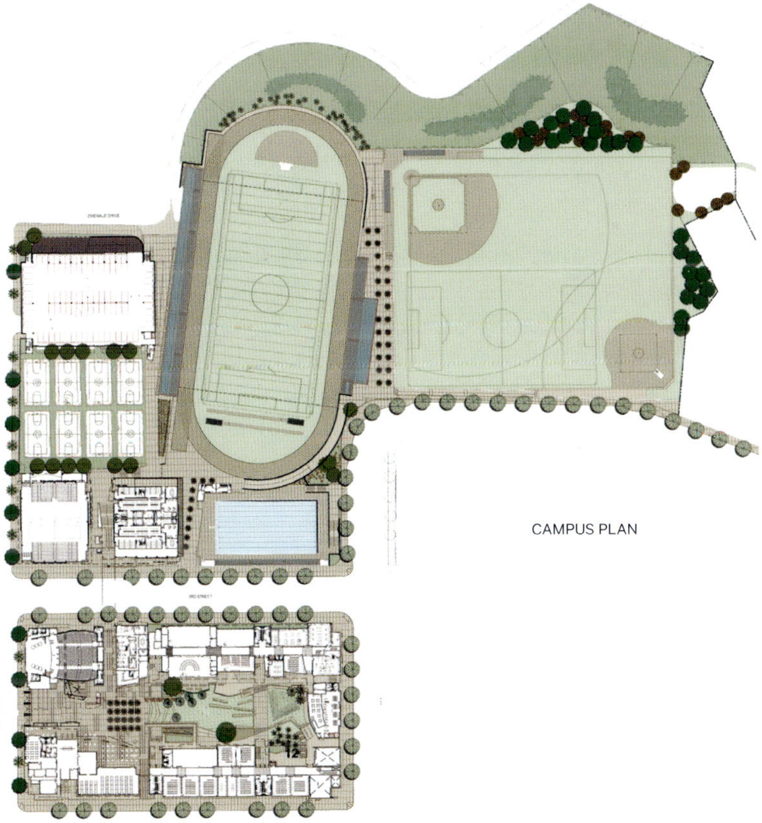

CAMPUS PLAN

The Roy Romer Middle School is located at the intersection of Laurel Canyon Boulevard and Hamlin Street in the San Fernando Valley. The site's surroundings include the 170 Freeway located a quarter-mile west of the site, commercial, and residential neighborhoods and air traffic from nearby Van Nuys and Burbank Airports. The L-shaped site is comprised of nine-and-a-half acres and is bounded by single-family residences to the west.

The new Middle School accommodates 1,600 students in 160,000 square feet of enclosed space. Campus buildings are organized around a large public square that serves as the school's entry and major outdoor social center. Accessed from Laurel Canyon Boulevard, the square is defined by a 97,000-square-foot Classroom and Administration wing to the north, a 25,000-square-foot, two-story multi-purpose building along the south, and a two-story 6,000-square-foot Multi-Media Center at the northwest corner. A fourth building, a 19,000-square-foot gymnasium, is located between parking and the playing field that extends from the plaza at the east to the westerly border of the site. The plan diagram for the project is a series of north-south building and landscape zones that create privacy and a variety of intimate spaces for small-group activity and instruction.

ROY ROMER MIDDLE SCHOOL
NORTH HOLLYWOOD, CALIFORNIA

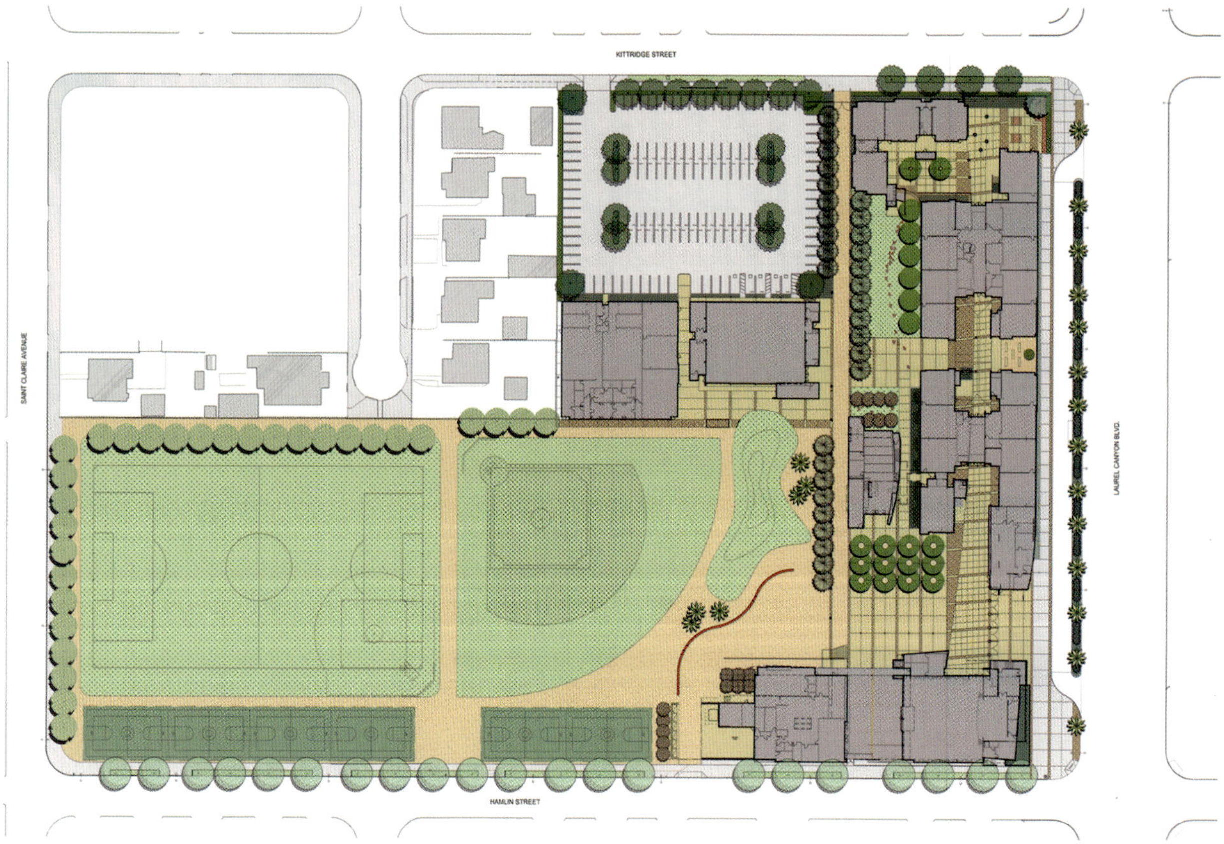

CAMPUS PLAN

ILLUSTRATIVE SITE PLAN

EXIT

TALL
CULTURE
COMMUNITY
CRAFT
HOME

Johnson Fain was commissioned to design Guild Lofts, a new mixed-use residential project containing 191 apartments in the historic Washington, DC Navy Yard. The bold and simple massing of the 200,000-square-foot building recalls the industrial scale and character of nearby historic ship-building structures. Large expanses of glass, perforated exterior shading panels, and rooftop clerestories maximize natural daylighting. The building's concrete frame is animated by a combination of clear glass, industrial window frames, and balconies. Amenities include a two-story social lounge and landscaped courtyard in addition to a rooftop garden with views of the Anacostia River. The ground level is populated with outboard retail stores and the interior public spaces sport a wide range of furnishings, fine arts installations, and graphic design.

GUILD LOFTS
WASHINGTON, D.C.

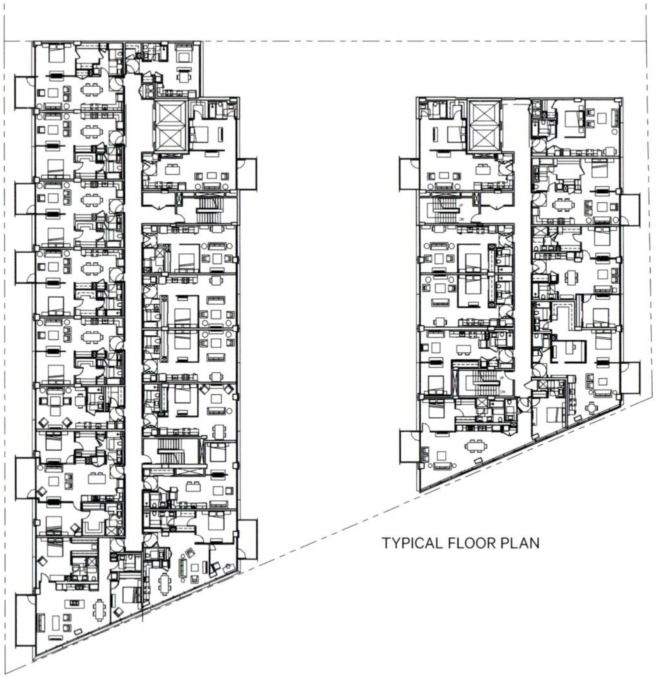

TYPICAL FLOOR PLAN

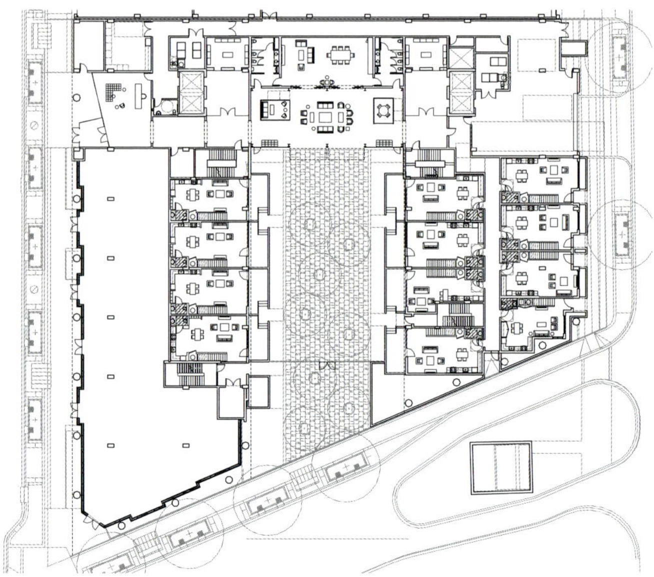

GROUND FLOOR PLAN

The new guild of
craftsman must get
back to the craft.
The ultimate aim of
all artistic activity
is building.
WALTER GROPIUS
900885 2

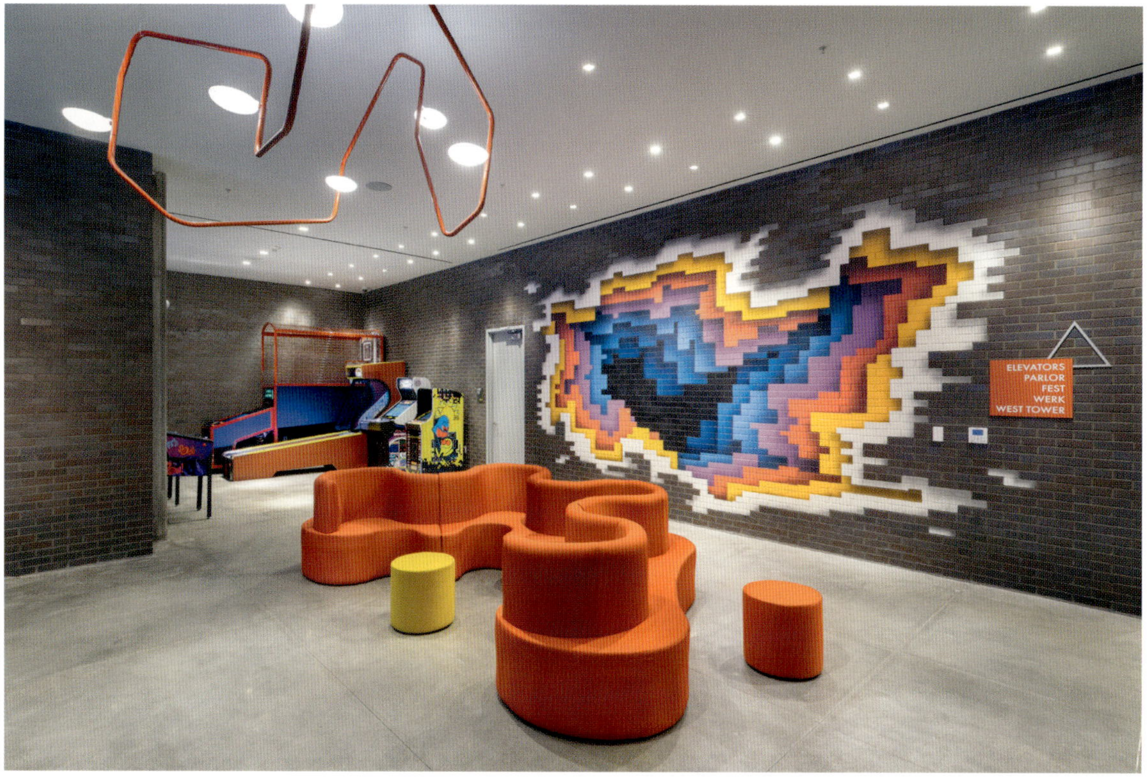
ELEVATORS
PARLOR
FEST
WERK
WEST TOWER

Metropolitan Lofts (MetLofts) in downtown Los Angeles is a unique "ground-up" residential loft building. A mixed-use development of 264 loft-style apartments, the project includes many amenities, ground-level live/work duplexes, 11,000 square feet of retail space, and parking. Located in the South Park District of downtown Los Angeles, MetLofts is adjacent to LA Live! and the Los Angeles Convention Center. Designed as a market-rate apartment project, 20% of the units meet affordability criteria. The project is the culmination of a redevelopment effort led by the former Community Redevelopment Authority to turn a once desolate city block of surface parking into a vibrant mixed-income residential community of affordable, senior, and family orientated residences with flats and townhomes for the physically challenged.

MetLofts features a landscaped interior courtyard with ground-level amenities visually open to other developments on the block and to pedestrians on 11th and Flower Streets. The lofts range in size from 690 to 1,400 square feet in one- and two-bedroom configurations. Also available are eleven street-level live/work units and studio apartments. Loft-like, each unit has large expanses of glass, high ceilings, open kitchens, and exposed structural and mechanical systems. Common amenities include a screening room, TV lounge, swimming pool, fitness center, and outdoor dining. A full building-height LED display connected to an interactive "welcome mat" at the building entry is the result of the work of the digital artist Electroland.

METROPOLITAN LOFTS
LOS ANGELES, CALIFORNIA

METLOFTS
URBAN
RENTAL
LIVING

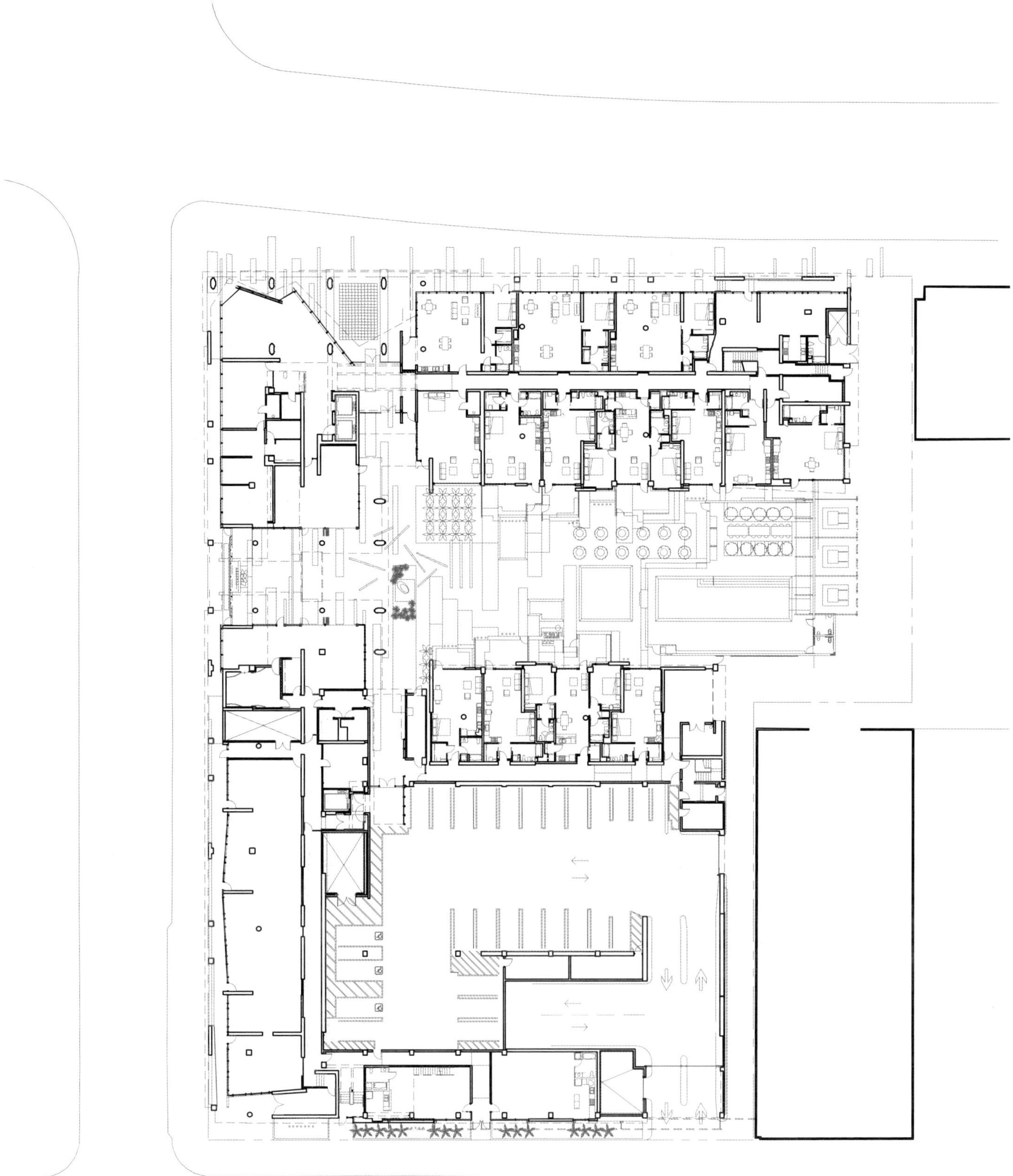

GROUND FLOOR PLAN

The character, scale, and ground level of Blossom Plaza were designed to connect Broadway, the main street for Los Angeles' Chinatown, to the nearby Metro Gold Line Station. This highly accessible and pedestrian-friendly network of public open spaces is animated with retail street frontages, a landscaped pedestrian promenade and architectural details that recall distinctive buildings in the neighborhood. The project includes 235 apartments above a mixed-use podium, 20% of which are dedicated as affordable housing and 20,000 square feet of ground-level space reserved for retail and food-and-beverage tenants. Generous public open space has been designed to accommodate neighborhood events and features paving patterns that reflect historic Chinese geometries. While contemporary, the building architecture incorporates bright colors, bold graphics, and selected details that reinforce the neighborhood's existing identity.

BLOSSOM PLAZA
LOS ANGELES, CALIFORNIA

BLOSSOM
PLAZA
金瑞龍城
Available
For Lease

LA Plaza Village is a low-rise, high-density project comprising two city blocks and a pedestrian paseo that connects the LA Plaza de Cultura y Artes Museum and the historic Pueblo with the foot of Fort Moore. Anchored by the Los Angeles headquarters of the Cesar Chavez Foundation, retail, food-and-beverage vending, cultural programming, and residences in a wide array of formats, the new project enriches a distinct neighborhood within the downtown core.

The Village contains 355 residential units, 20% of which qualify as affordable. The unit mix includes live/work lofts, studios, one-, two-, and three-bedroom family focused apartments. In addition to the ground level public open space, more than a dozen common roof decks provide settings for social interaction and recreation. State-of-the-art amenities include a large fitness center, swimming pool, and spa, dog park, and community lounge. A public arts program, interpretive signage and graphics, paving inlays, cultural iconography and traditional building materials honor the cultures that have come together to form this diverse downtown neighborhood.

LA PLAZA VILLAGE
LOS ANGELES, CALIFORNIA

SITE PLAN

LA BREA
TAR PITS
TAR
PITS
555

Runway at Playa Vista is the mixed-use commercial and social center of this new community. Centrally located and abutting Jefferson Boulevard, the project has been designed to contain Runway, a lively central "main street" that runs from McConnell Avenue to Village Drive. A wide array of retail anchors, in-line shops, and restaurants line Runway. A premium grocer and movie complex complete the retail program that totals nearly 200,000 square feet. A central tower with elevators, escalators, and a ground-floor plaza anchors the street and serves as a gateway between parking and the active streetscape. Three levels of creative office space totaling 25,000 square feet are located above the ground level with large expanses of glass and planted terraces that look onto the street.

Running north and south between Runway and Millennium Road is Town Center Drive, a short street lined with restaurants and cafes, widened sidewalks for outdoor dining, and canopies and trellises for shade and weather protection. Above the retail, 220 residential apartments with large windows, balconies, and articulated walls animate the streets. Recreational residential courtyards serving the residents sit atop the first retail floor. Restaurants wrap the corners of Town Center Drive and Millennium Road and mix with ground-floor two-story townhouses. Residential parking is located below grade.

RUNWAY AT PLAYA VISTA
PLAYA VISTA, CALIFORNIA

LYFE

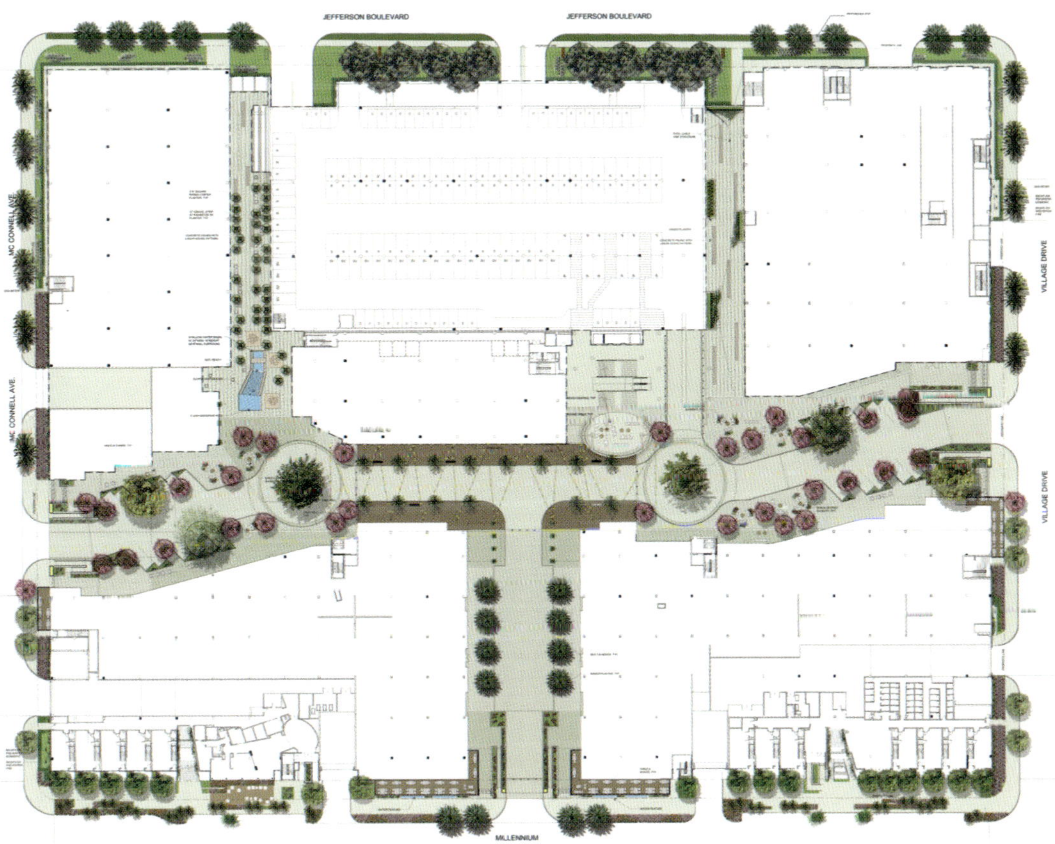
JEFFERSON BOULEVARD
JEFFERSON BOULEVARD
MC CONNELL AVE
MC CONNELL AVE
VILLAGE DRIVE
VILLAGE DRIVE
MILLENNIUM

SITE PLAN

at&t
LYFE KITCHEN

College Station, located on a five-and-a-half-acre site in downtown Los Angeles, lies at the intersection of College and Spring Streets at the top of the Alameda corridor. Three blocks north of Union Station and a five-minute walk to the center of Chinatown, the project is adjacent to the neighborhood Gold Line Metro station. College Station provides 715 apartments over a landscaped podium with 50,000 square feet of street-level retail, 37,000 square feet of which is a major grocer. The project incorporates four levels of parking, a two-story podium of retail, and five stories of residential apartments divided among five buildings.

Building facades along Spring and College Streets feature an array of vertical saw-tooth bay windows clad in varying tones of gray and silver metal panels that will shade glass and orient views toward the downtown skyline and the State Historic Park across the street. The site landscape has been designed to reflect the native vegetation of the nearby Los Angeles River and the park with view corridors from downtown to the San Gabriel Mountains.

COLLEGE STATION
LOS ANGELES, CALIFORNIA

THE
FARMERS
MARKET
Alameda St
North Spring St

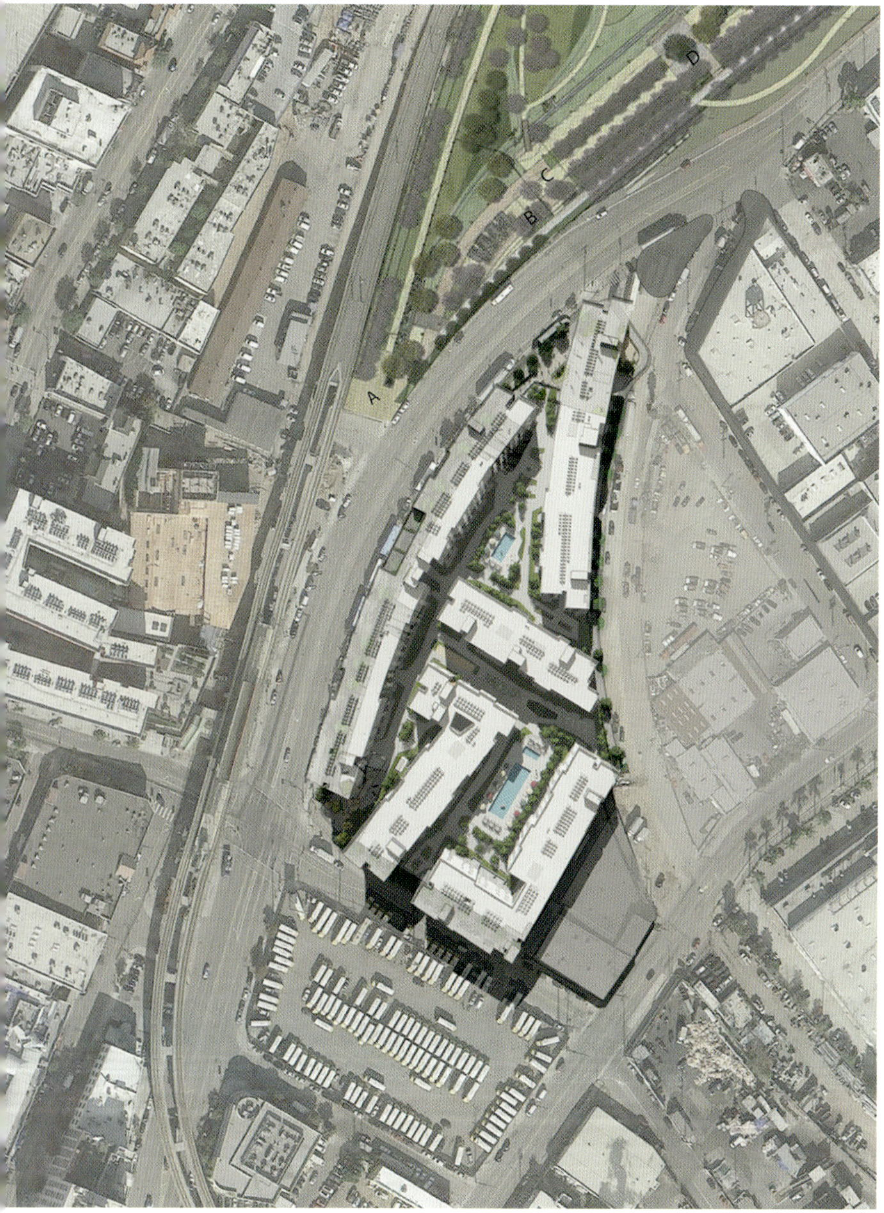

SITE PLAN

GROUND FLOOR PLAN

Citrus Commons is a new low-rise mixed-use project occupying the eight-acre site of the historic Sunkist headquarters building in Sherman Oaks, California. The project design restores the landmark modernist building, pays tribute to the region's agricultural heritage, and integrates it into a pedestrian-centric urban village. The historic 168,000-square-foot office building is re-imaged as a creative office environment, surrounded by gardens and outdoor gathering spaces and centered on the historic central atrium, replanted and refurnished.

Two new mixed-use residential buildings will be built along the major thoroughfare of Riverside Drive to the north. The project will include 45,000 square feet of retail. A major grocer will anchor the ground floor on Riverside Drive along with smaller adjacent retail tenants and a residential lobby. Two hundred and fifty residential units will include a mix of one and two bedroom units with ground-level townhouses fronting Riverside Drive. Parking is provided for 565 cars on two below-grade levels and in two above-grade parking structures. Street trees and furnishings, paving, and plant materials will provide continuity and encourage public access through the project, the surrounding neighborhoods and the landscaped parkway along the adjacent Los Angeles River.

CITRUS COMMONS
SHERMAN OAKS, CALIFORNIA

Terrace Theater

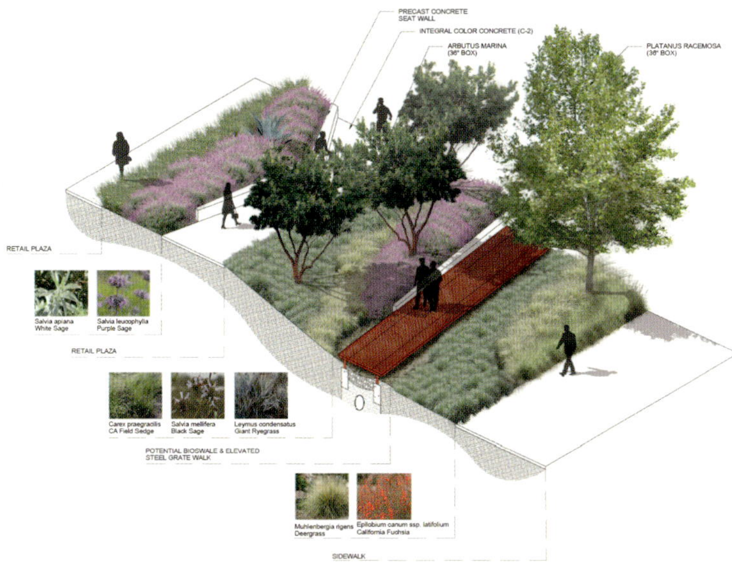
PRECAST CONCRETE
SEAT WALL
INTEGRAL COLOR CONCRETE (C-2)
ARBUTUS MARINA
(36" BOX)
PLATANUS RACEMOSA
(36" BOX)
RETAIL PLAZA
Salvia apiana
White Sage
Salvia leucophylla
Purple Sage
RETAIL PLAZA
Carex praegracilis
CA Field Sedge
Salvia mellifera
Black Sage
Leymus condensatus
Giant Ryegrass
POTENTIAL BIOSWALE & ELEVATED
STEEL GRATE WALK
Muhlenbergia rigens
Deergrass
Epilobium canum ssp. latifolium
California Fuchsia
SIDEWALK

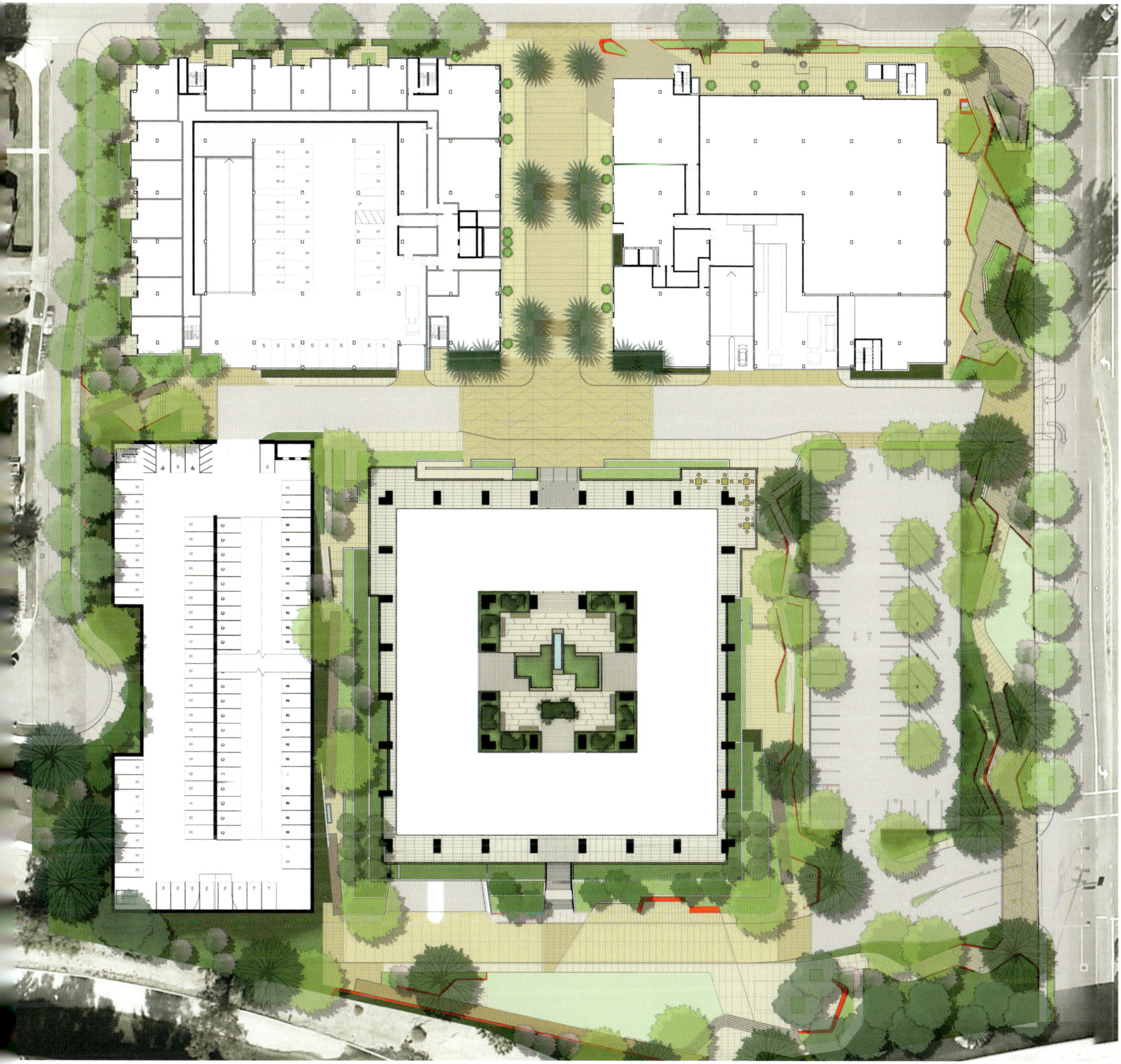

SITE PLAN

TALL
CULTURE
COMMUNITY
CRAFT
HOME

Johnson Fain was recently commissioned to design a 58,000-square-foot expansion to the Opus One Winery in the Napa Valley. The enhancements include an exclusive VIP Tasting Room, an intimate Reserve Library looking into the Grand Chai where first-year barrels are on display, public tasting rooms that open to a veranda, new production spaces and administrative offices. The design team took inspiration from the original design, completed by Johnson Fain in 1989, while creating fresh opportunities to revisit the singular vineyard setting. Design elements reflect a unity of winemaking, food, and artful living.

Interior design elements of the new upper-level Partners' Room include fossilized stone floors, cream-colored limestone walls, and a textured rough-sawn hemlock ceiling that continues from the interior to the outside veranda. Exterior walls are designed with floor-to-ceiling glass to maximize the views to the vineyard and the Napa Valley landscape beyond. Skylights bring soft light into the interior space that features walnut millwork, blackened steel, and bronze accents and clear glass. Joan Behnke & Associates collaborated on the interior design and furnishings.

OPUS ONE WINERY
OAKVILLE, CALIFORNIA

AETNA SPRINGS CLUBHOUSE
POPE VALLEY, CALIFORNIA

Johnson Fain was commissioned to provide visioning and architectural design services to restore the historic Napa Valley-based Aetna Springs as a premier resort. The new 8,800-square-foot golf clubhouse recalls the quintessential North Bay style, relying heavily on wood construction that reflects the highly detailed craftspersonship of the late 19th and early 20th centuries. The clubhouse offers state-of-the-art amenities while preserving the character of the legendary resort and a bygone era. Taking cues from the Bernard Maybeck-designed Dining Hall on the site, the clubhouse features large, exposed wood trusses, stone columns, fireplaces, and generously scaled chandeliers. The sweeping verandas and expansive glass walls provide natural light and panoramic views of the restored historic golf course and the rolling hills surrounding the northern Napa County property. Inventive details and a rich array of materials provide the clubhouse with a distinctive and consistent character.

The clubhouse's materials, structure, and siting celebrate the historic golf course and the area's natural beauty. Working with Johnson Fain, renowned golf course designer Tom Doak meticulously restored the original nine-hole course, the oldest on the West Coast. The two-story clubhouse contains a main dining hall, lounge, bar, pro shop, and locker rooms, and is the social center of this restored resort community.

ÆTNA

A sweeping, curved roof, reminiscent of the rolling hills surrounding the site, is the central feature of the Byron Winery. In keeping with California's experimental tradition, the 32,000-square-foot Byron Winery is both strikingly futuristic and respectful of the land from which it grows. Built from natural materials, the winery is formed of cedar planks, steel windows, and zinc sheet roofing. Highlighted by free-form plaster panels of intense earth pigments, a long, shaded portico runs the length of the building, providing entry to the tasting and barrel rooms and a panoramic view of the vineyards below.

The project's technical features include 10,000 square feet of barrel-aging facilities, with a cave-like environment for optimal humidity and temperature control, gravity-flow design, state-of-the-art technology including specially designed grape sorting tables, and portable tank transport systems. A tasting room, catering kitchen and wine library are also included. The winery is sited on 640 acres of vineyards and maintains an annual production of 70,000 cases.

BYRON WINERY
NORTHERN SANTA BARBARA COUNTY, CALIFORNIA

Johnson Fain was commissioned to design a 5,000-square-foot restaurant, kitchen, and patio for Michelin Star chef Tony Esnault's and restauranteur Yassmin Sarmadi's new French restaurant, Knife Pleat, at the notable Orange County fashion destination, South Coast Plaza. Johnson Fain designed and developed the architecture, interiors, and furnishings from concept design through construction. The design team took inspiration from the aptly named Knife Pleat, which is a nod to the intermingling of the culinary and fashion worlds, looking to the classic fashion designers for visual themes: Chanel, Dior, and Balenciaga.

The palette is muted with a few dramatic accents, the silhouettes are soft yet structured and the style evokes classic detailing. Exterior design elements include a storefront comprised of backlit, translucent white onyx walls with polished brass inlays, and large sliding doors of custom patterned glass that open up the restaurant to connect the main dining area to the skylit shopping center. The outdoor dining patio features limestone walls, a full-height garden wall, and a metal and wood trellis. Interior features include a dining area anchored by a feature bar made of fluted cast stone and brass with a veined Calacatta marble top fronting an open kitchen. The main dining room features a large, custom brass and translucent glass light fixture that branches out over the room.

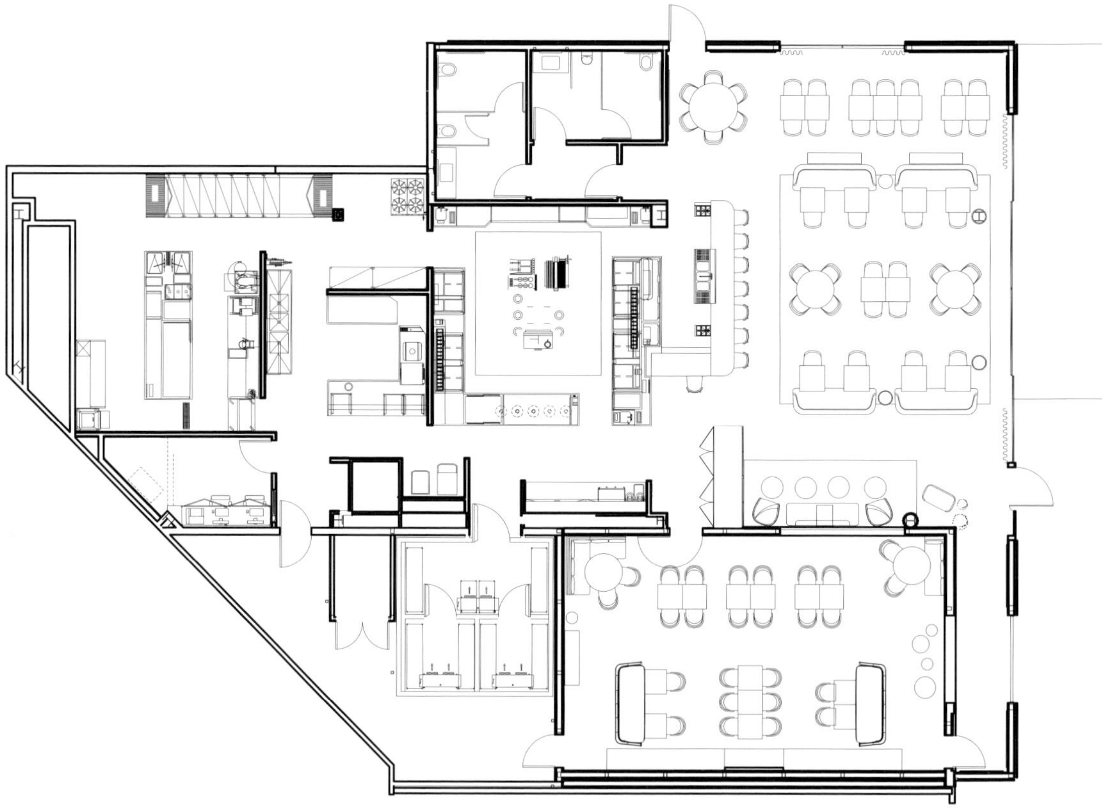

FLOOR PLAN

KNIFE PLEAT
COSTA MESA, CALIFORNIA

The Country Club at Sandy Lane encompasses 55,000 square feet of hospitality space and is located on a hillside overlooking golf and the west coast of Barbados. A large, cobbled motor court surrounded by a garden arcade leads up to the building. The entry is located in a tall, conical vestibule that recalls the historic sugar mills from the island's agricultural past. The building's exterior is dressed in bands of coral plaster and sanded Portuguese limestone. Primary lounges and the principal restaurant and bar are shaded by a deep radial soffit that protects guests and golfers from the hot tropical sun and allows the building to naturally ventilate by virtue of the area's frequent trade winds. Views to the Sandy Lane and Green Monkey golf courses, both designed by Tom Fazio, and to the coastline beyond, are wide and unobstructed.

Both the golf pro shop and the member's lounge are designed as circular forms to maximize wide views of the tropical landscape. Administration space and the men's and women's locker rooms are rectangular in form, flank the public space, and help to form the arcaded motor court. A golf cart maintenance facility and barn, as well as employee facilities, storage, and support spaces are on the basement floor. Interior finishes in the public areas include hand-troweled coral, cement plaster, marble, and limestone, and interior millwork is executed in dark, farmed mahogany. The floor paving is designed in two shades of honed travertine with large geometric patterns that extend out into the landscape.

SANDY LANE GOLF CLUBHOUSE
ST. JAMES PARISH, BARBADOS

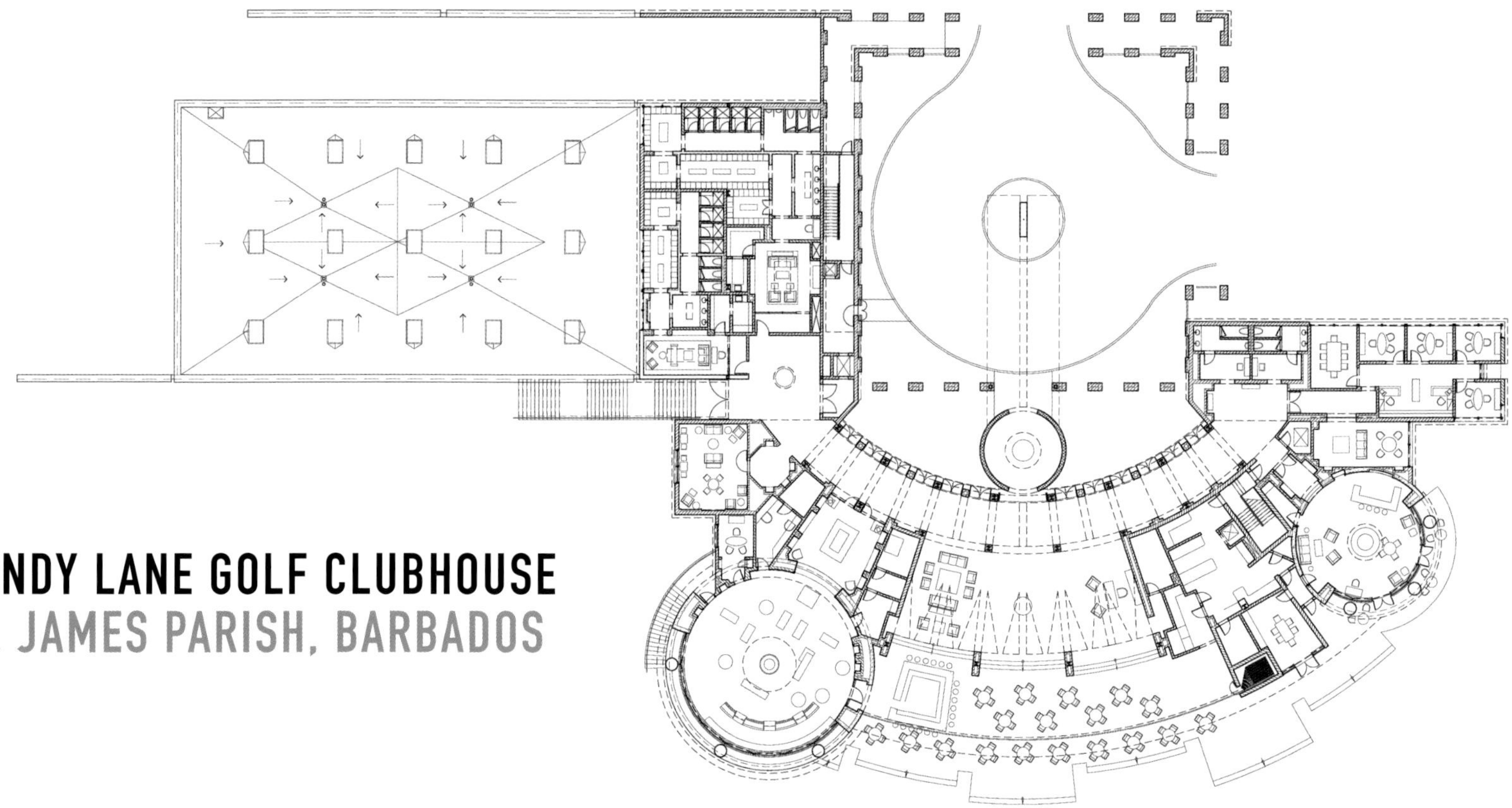

GROUND FLOOR PLAN

GREAT WALL WINERY AND VISITOR CENTER
HEBEI PROVINCE, CHINA

The new buildings at the Great Wall Winery and Visitors Center in Hebei province, China are located at the top of an expansive vineyard and adjacent to the existing winery originally founded in the mid-1980s. Johnson Fain was commissioned to design a new 140,000-square-foot central winery complex that connects the old buildings to the new, provides a comprehensive space for a new winery tour and showcases winemaking, banquet, and conference spaces including 60 deluxe guest rooms and hospitality support facilities. The configuration of the building plan was designed to follow the topography of the sloping terrain and to position the floor levels so that the connection between the new Visitors Center and the pre-existing buildings occurs all at one level without grade changes. This effort results in a long and serpentine architecture with corniced roofline that is perfectly level and horizontal against the background of rolling vineyards.

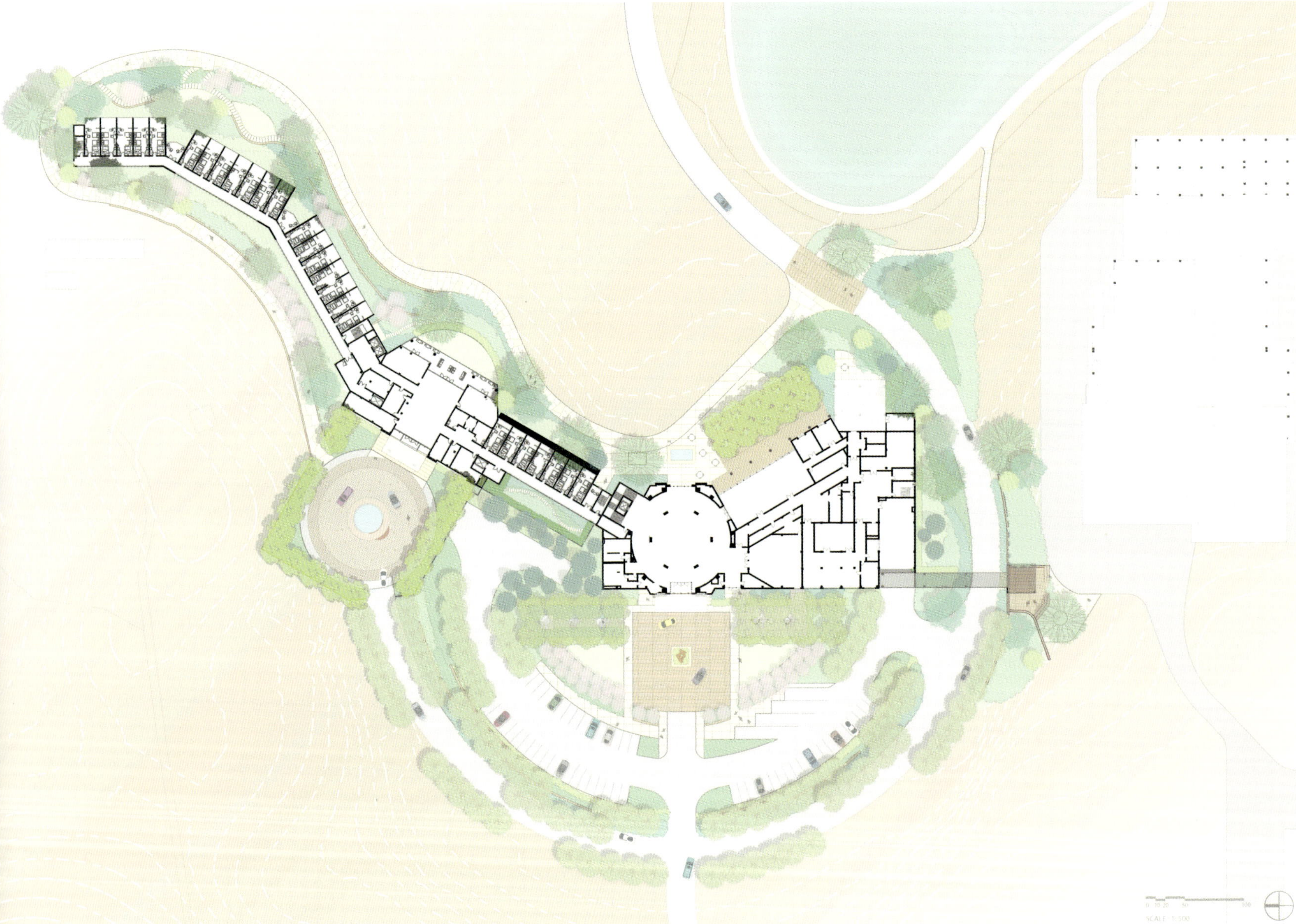

SITE PLAN

TALL

CULTURE

COMMUNITY

CRAFT

HOME

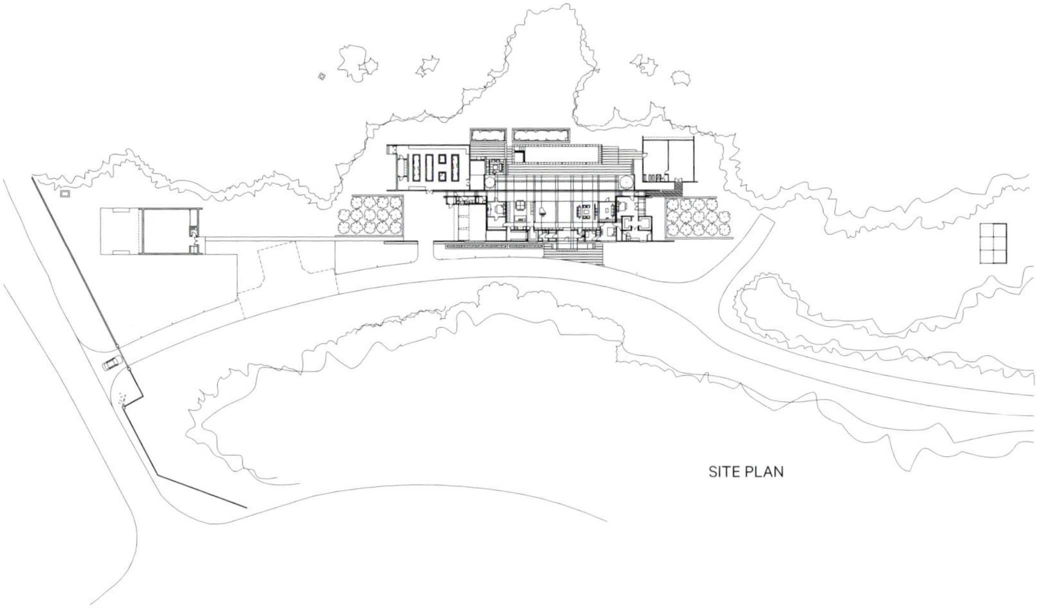

SITE PLAN

This 6,000-square-foot private residence was designed for a 12-acre site at the western edge of the Ojai Valley. Accessed by a private road, the home is sited in an open meadow surrounded by groves of native oak trees. Designed for an extended family, three outbuildings have been added to the principal home: a guesthouse and dance studio, a painting studio, and a performance shed for outdoor activities. The home's living room is designed for music recitals with an elevated plinth and grand piano at one end and a seating group at the other, surrounding a fireplace. Stone planters contain native plantings while the majority of the land is left natural and groomed. Adjacent to the kitchen is an organic food garden and the home is book-ended by peach and apricot orchards.

The rooftop of the main building has a large photovoltaic array as well as a rainwater harvesting system. The westerly exterior wall has been designed as a thermally separated rain screen system insulating the interior of the house from solar heat gain, and select floors include radiant cooling and heating. The home is naturally ventilated both horizontally and vertically with screens and automated clerestories.

WALL HOUSE
OJAI, CALIFORNIA

This 4,500-square-foot single-story home is located in the Napa Valley above the Silverado Trail. The house sits at the top of a 42-acre site accessed by a private road with a vineyard below. The house has been designed as a weekend home and office for a couple, as well as a place for entertaining and overseeing a new winery venture. The primary massing is a highly ordered series of rectangular volumes clad in precisely finished steel panels. The house is designed to be an integral part of its natural surroundings with elements such as a central living space composed of glass walls that provide a uniquely framed view out to the landscape and slender steel columns and concrete piers that support exposed wood soffits and mirror the many native trees on the site.

The interior material palette ranges from simple plywood ceilings and polished concrete floors to the rich texture of cleft quartzite stone stairs and glass mosaic tiled floors and walls. Interior walls are veneered natural-tone plaster. Living spaces are further defined by maple-veneered suspended ceilings beneath exposed wooden roof joists. Millwork elements are custom-designed and composed of ebonized and stained maple veneers, brushed stainless steel, and silver travertine. The landscape design includes stepped terraces, a lap pool, spa, barbecue, and an exterior fireplace set within the natural landscape of boulders and native oak trees.

BRIDGE HOUSE
RUTHERFORD, CALIFORNIA

This home is located on White Sulphur Springs Road six miles west of Main Street, Saint Helena, in the Napa Valley. Sited one thousand feet above the valley floor, the house sits on 60 acres of wilderness that borders California State parkland and Iron Mine Creek. The house is sited immediately above a hillside vineyard facing the valley to the east. The driveway is located in a grove of native oaks, and the entrance to the house is marked by a 200-foot-long uninterrupted wall that extends into the home. Beginning at the driveway, the wall passes through the entrance and down into a central gallery, culminating in a living room defined by three walls of glass and two flanking fireplaces. Circulation throughout the house is informally defined by a series of stone steps and landings that follow the descent of the hill and form the basis of the plan. Over the length of the house, four glazed thresholds separate the longitudinal procession of the building with floor-to-ceiling glass lites, capturing views of the landscape left and right.

Finishes in the house are elemental. The exterior is clad in wide, horizontal, rough-sawn cedar planks weathered gray with steel windows and door frames. On the interior, sandblasted plywood panels, plastered walls, cedar doors, slate counter tops, and glass mosaic tiles are employed throughout.

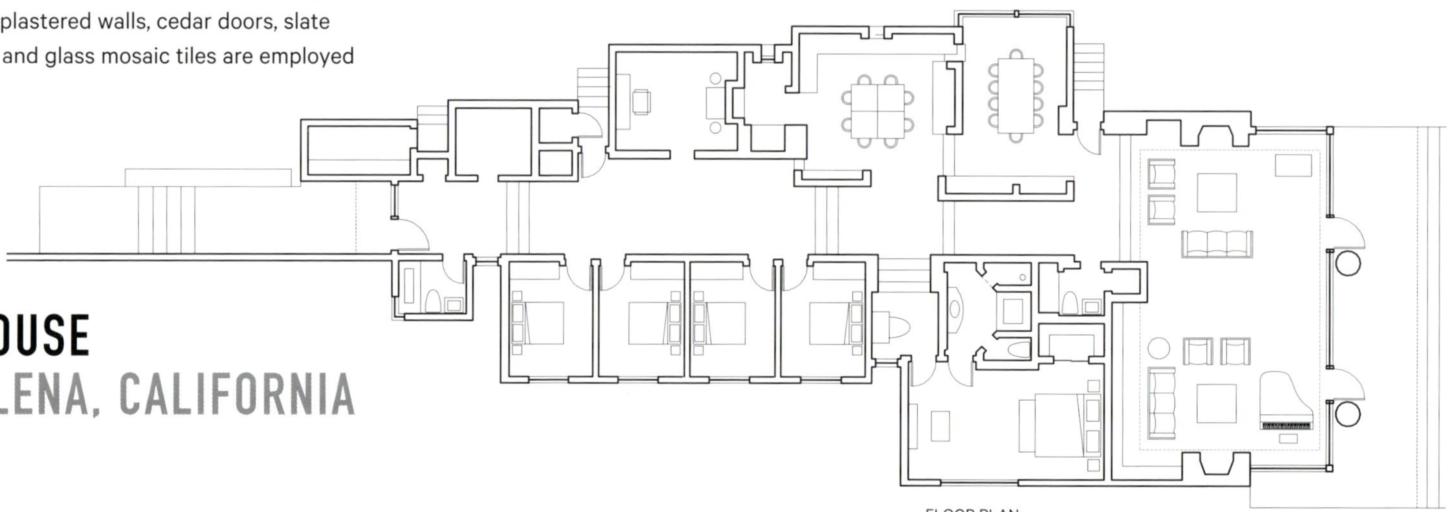

FLOOR PLAN

BOX HOUSE
ST. HELENA, CALIFORNIA

FRAME HOUSE
LOS ALTOS HILLS, CALIFORNIA

This 6,800-square-foot, one-story home is located at the southern end of the San Francisco Bay on a 12-acre hilltop site overlooking Silicon Valley. The project represents a substantial expansion and remodel of an important mid-century modern house designed in the mid-1950s by the architect John Funk, and featured in Sally Woodbridge's seminal book Bay Area Houses. The house had fallen into disrepair prior to its acquisition.

The design preserves all primary steel structure and window frames, the principal ceiling plane, and the radiant concrete floor slab that ran throughout the original house. The building was then expanded to accommodate the activities of a young and growing family of five. Accordingly, kitchen and dining spaces were enlarged at the perimeter of the building envelope where natural daylight could be maximized.

Deep overhangs protect expansive glass walls from solar heat gain while large operable panes allow ample cross ventilation in concert with radiant floors to provide a completely passive heating and cooling system. New skylight monitors in the roof bring natural light into the interior of the house. Play rooms and study spaces have been introduced at both ends of the original home to allow parental proximity to young children throughout. The original bedroom wing was expanded to include interior wardrobe and storage as well as expanded bath and dressing areas.

LOCAL COLOR

DRUM HOUSE
MALIBU, CALIFORNIA

This hillside home was designed for a family of five and is located on a sloping site overlooking the Pacific Ocean. The 8,000-square-foot structure is set into the hillside with motor court and primary entry on the top of two floors. A dramatic and skylit stair lines the interior of a fully glazed and cylindrical two-story living room. All primary rooms are fully glazed to the west giving them ocean views and maximizing sunlight and fresh air.

All bedrooms, including the master suite, are located on the upper level with living, dining, kitchen, and breakfast rooms at grade with direct access to a broad terrace with swimming pool and spa. A pre-existing 4,000-square-foot house on the site has been remodeled and connected to the new building and functions as a guesthouse and studio.

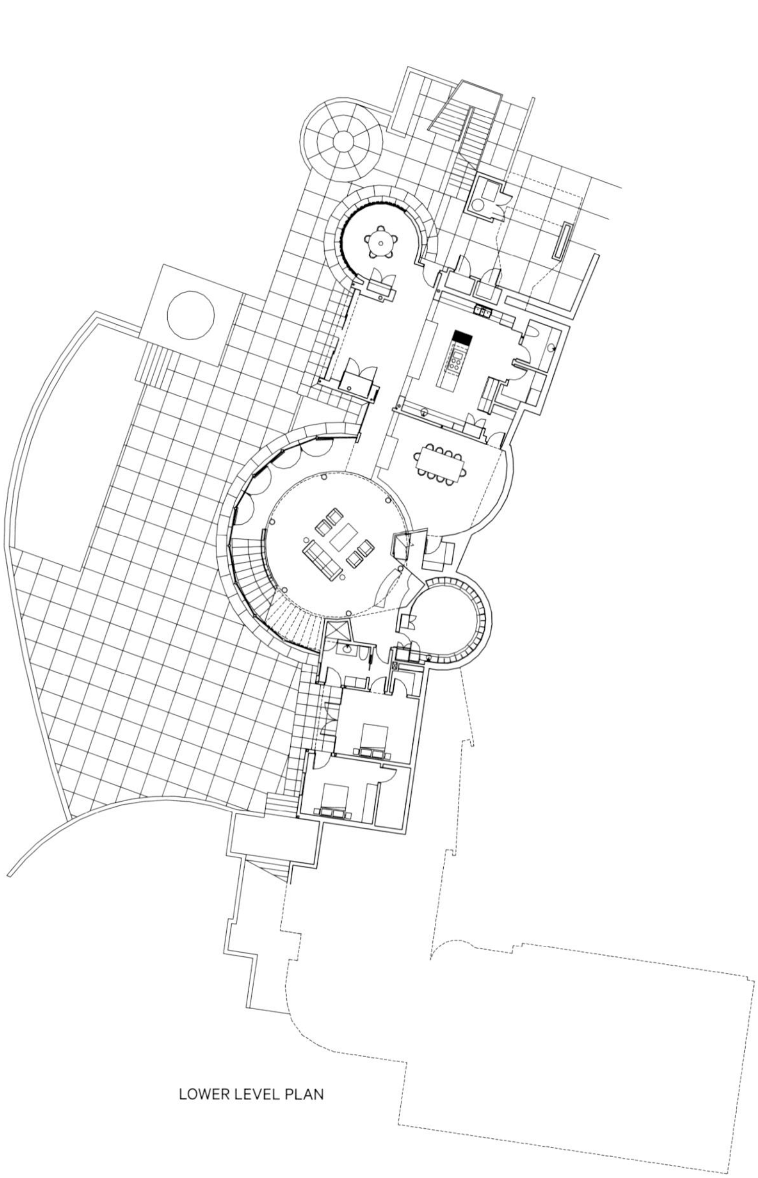

LOWER LEVEL PLAN

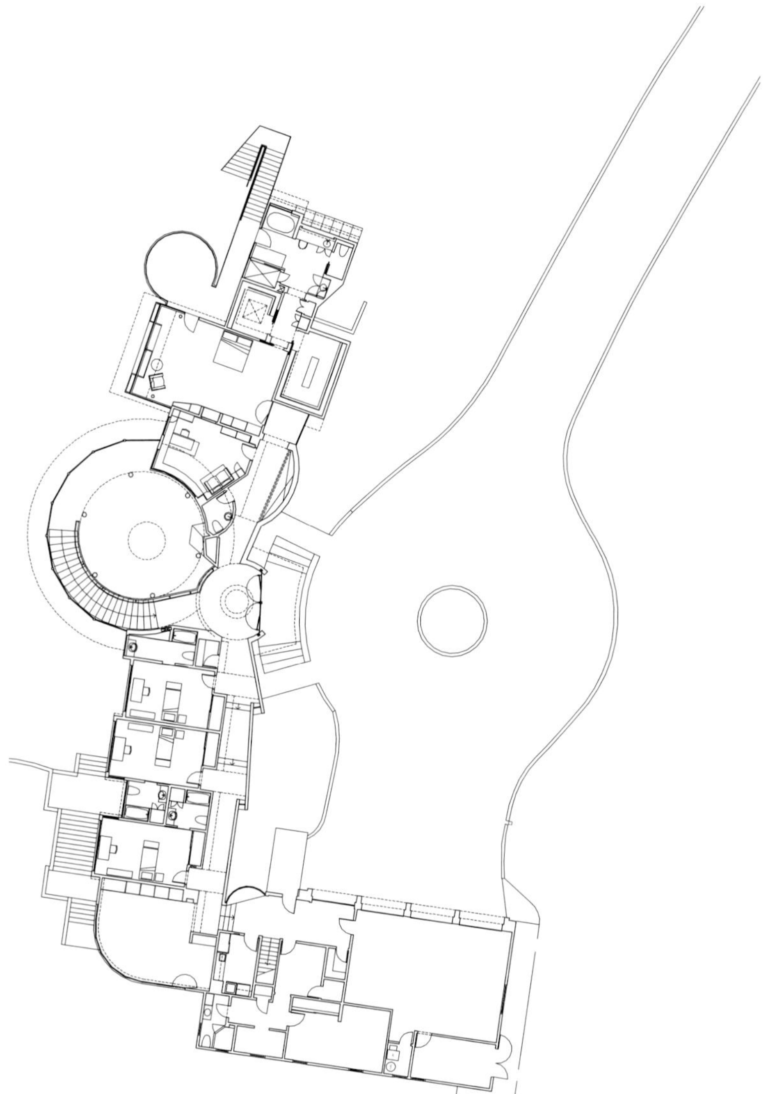

UPPER LEVEL PLAN

INSIDE/OUTSIDE HOUSE
BEVERLY HILLS, CALIFORNIA

This new 6,000-square-foot single-story home is located in the Trousdale Estates on the hillside above Beverly Hills. The neighborhood, largely built out in the 1950s and '60s, is notable for its range of mid-century modern houses. The original building was demolished to the ground and rebuilt. The main house and guest facilities are connected by broad overhangs that shelter outdoor activities from the sun and frame expansive views of the Los Angeles basin below. Twelve floor-to-ceiling glass panels on the southern side of the common areas slide to fully open the home's interior to the outside. The rear yard features a zero-edge swimming pool and spa, outdoor kitchen, barbecue, and fire pit.

The interior of the house contains three bedrooms, five bathrooms, a media room, bar, office, sauna and steam room, and a three-car garage. The finish palette is restrained with polished concrete floors, blackened iron millwork, and quarter-sawn Douglas fir ceilings and walls. A central clerestory runs the length of the house bringing in natural light and connecting the common areas of the open plan.

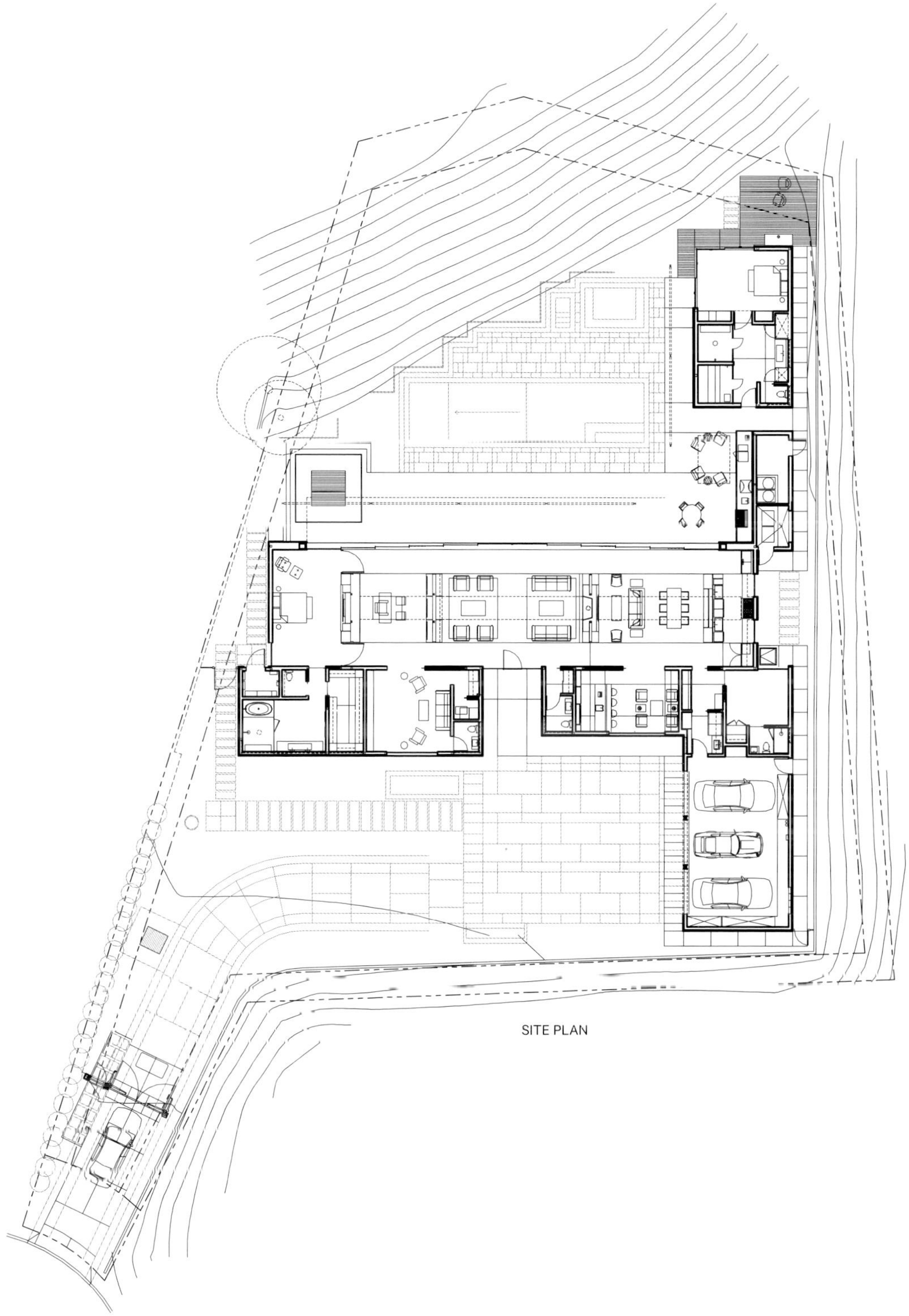

SITE PLAN

This three-story, 5,000-square-foot urban townhouse is built on a low-rise commercial street in central Los Angeles surrounded by large historic homes. The family of four wished to live within walking distance of commercial services in a mixed-use urban environment to reduce automobile dependence. The exterior facade is composed of corrugated steel panels and a custom glass curtain wall. Precision has been achieved through the manipulation of these two material systems into pure geometric forms, expressing both the inner workings of the house, and avoiding the formal language of the traditional single-family dwelling.

The ground-floor provides space for laundry, housekeeping, utilities, and a large room facing an enclosed garden used by the children for media and music. A shelter for automobiles is tucked under the slab of the second floor. Compact urban gardens exist on three sides of the house: flower and kitchen garden to the rear, an outdoor room with canopy trees and a hedgerow wall for privacy to the front, and winter vegetable garden to the south. The second floor is the primary activity floor with living and dining rooms, kitchen, a private patio, swimming pool, and the master bedroom suite. The third floor includes a library and children's bedrooms. With the exceptions of individual bedrooms, all spaces interconnect horizontally and vertically, opening up the house and maximizing shared space.

LARCHMONT BOULEVARD TOWNHOUSE
LOS ANGELES, CALIFORNIA

429 N

CLEANER

Designed for a professional couple that relocated to the emerging Arts District in downtown Los Angeles, this 2,300-square-foot loft residence enjoys a two-story-tall volume with a second level mezzanine remodeled to include an office, full bath, guest bedroom, and wardrobe. At the ground level the open plan includes a living area, grand piano, open galley kitchen and dining, and the master bedroom area. All bathrooms, closets, and the powder room are otherwise enclosed. The condominium is furnished to accommodate the couple, their visiting family, small groups, and large parties. A flower and herb garden serves as both an entrance and a patio for outdoor work and dining.

NATIONAL BISCUIT COMPANY LOFT
LOS ANGELES, CALIFORNIA

Johnson Fain Studio
Los Angeles, California

APPENDIX

SELECTED WORKS : PROJECT DATA

TALL

Museum Tower
Dallas, Texas
Completed 2013
113 Residences
Client: Brook Partners Inc; Turtle Creek Holdings; Criswell Radovan
Contractor: Turner Construction
Structural engineer: L.A. Fuess & Partners
MEP engineer: Blum Consulting Engineers
Landscape architect: Melendrez; SMR Landscape Architects, Inc
Executive Architect: Gromatzky Dupree & Associates
Interior Architects: Hirsch Bedner Associates; Booziotis & Company; Bodron + Fruit

Century City Center
Century City, California
Completed: 2025
1,605,500 sq. ft.
Client: JMB Realty
Contractor: Clark Construction
Structural engineer: Nabih Youssef Structural Engineers
MEP engineer: Arup
Landscape architect: OJB

Solitaire
Taichung City, Taiwan
Completed: 2015
150 Residences
Client: Pao Huei Development
Contractor: Shu Ming Construction Co., Ltd.
Landscape architect: Landworks Studio
Interior Designer: Hirsh-Bedner Associates

SkyTower
Taichung City, Taiwan
Completed 2023
100 Residences
Client: Pao Huei Development
Contractor: Shu Ming Construction Co., Ltd.
Landscape architect: Landworks Studio
Interior Designer: Hirsh-Bedner Associates

City Park
Taichung City, Taiwan
Completed: 2021
96 Residences
Client: Pao Huei Development
Contractor: Shu Ming Construction Co., Ltd.
Landscape architect: Landworks Studio
Interior Designer: Hirsh-Bedner Associates

Nantun
Taichung City, Taiwan
Completed: 2018
85 Residences
Client: Pao Huei Development
Contractor: Shu Ming Construction Co., Ltd.
Landscape architect: Landworks Studio
Interior Designer: Hirsh-Bedner Associates

Verde II
Jakarta, Indonesia
Completed: 2019
303 Residences
Client: PT. FarPoint Reality Indonesia
Contractor: PT. Total Bangun Persada Tbk.
Structural engineer: WHL – Archasia Consultants and Biro Design Wardhana
MEP engineer: Hantaran Prima Mandiri
Landscape architect: SWA Group & Citrapesona Hijau
Interior Architect: Yabu Pushelberg

Figueroa Eight
Los Angeles, California
Completed: 2023
438 Residences
Client: Mitsui Fudosan America
Contractor: Lendlease
Structural engineer: Englekirk Structural Engineers
MEP engineer: Glumac
Landscape architect: Relm
Executive Architect: HKS

6400 Sunset Boulevard
Hollywood, California
Completed: Entitlement
200 Residences
Client: GPI
Structural engineer: Nabih Youssef
MEP engineer: Glumac
Landscape architect: Studio MLA

Constellation Place
Century City, California
Completed 2003
704,000 sq. ft.
Client: JMB Realty
Contractor: Hathaway Dinwiddie
Structural engineer: WHL Consulting Engineers
MEP engineer: Levine Seegel Associates
Landscape architect: Studio MLA

CULTURE

First Americans Museum
Oklahoma City, Oklahoma
Completed 2021
177,974 sq. ft.
Client: Native American Cultural and Educational Authority
Contractor: Centennial Builders
Associate architect: Hornbeek Blatt Architects
Structural engineer: Nabih Youssef Associates
Civil engineer: Cardinal Engineering, Inc.
MEP engineer: IBE Consulting Engineers, Inc.
Landscape architect: Hargreaves Associates
Institutional planning: Lord Cultural Resources
Exhibit design: Ralph Appelbaum Associates

Christ Cathedral
Garden Grove, California
Completed 2019
79,000 sq. ft.
Client: Roman Catholic Diocese of Orange
Contractor: Synder Langston
Structural engineer: Nabih Youssef
MEP engineer: Syska & Hennessy, Inc.
Landscape architect: Rios Clementi Hale Studios

Capitol Area East End Complex
Sacramento, California
Completed 2003
1,500,000 sq. ft.
Client: State of California, Department of General Services
Contractor: Clark Construction Group, LLC and Hensel Phelps Construction Company
Associate architects: Gruen Architects, Fentress Bradburn Architects, Dreyfuss & Blackford Architects, SMWM Architects, and Forrar Williams Architects
Structural engineer: Middlebrook + Louie
MP engineer: Capital Engineering
Electrical engineer: Levine Seegel Associates
Landscape architect: Melendrez

Solano County Government Center
Fairfield, California
Completed 2005
300,000 sq. ft.
Client: County of Solano
Contractor: Clark Construction Group, LLC
Structural engineer: Nabih Youssef Associates
MP engineer: Capital Engineering Consultants
Electrical engineer: Levine Seegel Associates
Landscape architect: Melendrez

BioMarin
San Rafael, California
Completed: 2025
207,000 sq. ft.
Client: BioMarin Pharmaceutical, Inc
Contractor: Hathaway Dinwiddie
Structural engineer: Nabih Youssef and Associates
MEP engineer: Glumac
Landscape architect: MPA Design
Lab Design Consultant: GL Planning and Design

Genentech Building 31
South San Francisco, California
Completed 2014
130,000 sq. ft.
Client: Genentech
Contractor: Hathaway Dinwiddie
Structural engineer: Nabih Youssef Associates
Electrical engineer: KCA Engineers
Landscape architect: MPA Design

Genentech Building 32
South San Francisco, California
Completed 2004
125,387 sq. ft.
Client: Genentech
Contractor: Hathaway Dinwiddie
Structural engineer: Nabih Youssef Associates
Electrical engineer: KCA Engineers
Landscape architect: MPA Design

Genentech Building 33
South San Francisco, California
Completed 2005
130,115 sq. ft.
Client: Genentech
Contractor: Hathaway Dinwiddie
Structural engineer: Nabih Youssef Associates
Landscape architect: MPA Design

Amgen Center Building 27
Thousand Oaks, California
Completed 1997
230,000 sq. ft.
Client: Amgen
Contractor: Hathaway Dinwiddie
Structural engineer: Nabih Youssef Associates
MEP engineer: Levine Seegel Associates
Landscape architect: Melendrez

Amgen Center Building 30
Thousand Oaks, California
Completed 2000
360,000 sq. ft.
Client: Amgen
Contractor: Hathaway Dinwiddie
Structural engineer: KPFF Consulting Engineers
MEP engineer: Bechtel Industrial and Affiliated Engineers, Inc.
Landscape architect: Melendrez
Lab planner: FLAD

Amgen Center Building 38
Thousand Oaks, California
Completed 2000
265,000 sq. ft.
Client: Amgen
Contractor: Hathaway Dinwiddie
Structural engineer: Nabih Youssef Associates
MEP engineer: Levine Seegel Associates
Landscape architect: Melendrez

Sutardja Dai Hall
University of California, Berkeley
Completed 2009
141,000 sq. ft.
Client: University of California, Berkeley
Contractor: Hathaway Dinwiddie
Associate architect: SmithGroup
Structural engineer: Forell/Elsesser Engineers, Inc.
MEP engineer: Bard, Rao + Athanas Consulting Engineers, LLC
Landscape architect: KenKay Associates

Cal IT^2
University of California, Irvine
Completed 2004
120,000 sq. ft.
Client: University of California, Irvine
Contractor: PCL Construction Services
Associate architect: Leo A. Daly
Structural engineer: Nabih Youssef Associates
MP engineer: Capital Engineering
Electrical engineer: Levine Seegel Associates
Landscape architect: Melendrez

Miguel Contreras Learning Center
Los Angeles, California
Completed 2008
221,000 sq. ft.
Client: Los Angeles Unified School District
Contractor: Clark Construction Group, LLC
Structural engineer: Nabih Youssef Associates
MP engineer: William J. Yang & Associates
Electrical engineer: Silver, Roth & Associate, Inc.
Landscape architect: Mia Lehrer + Associates

Roy Romer Middle School
North Hollywood, California
Completed 2008
160,000 sq. ft.
Client: Los Angeles Unified School District
Contractor: Bernards
Structural engineer: Nabih Youssef Associates
MP engineer: William J. Yang & Associates
Electrical engineer: Silver, Roth & Associate, Inc.
Landscape architect: Mia Lehrer + Associates

COMMUNITY

Guild Lofts
Washington D.C.
Completed: 2018
191 Residences
Client: Forest City Enterprises
Contractor: Clark Construction Group, LLC
Structural engineer: SK&A Structural Engineers, PLLC
MEP engineer: Jordan & Skala Engineers
Landscape architect: Parker Rodriguez
Executive Architect: WDG Architecture

Metropolitan Lofts
Los Angeles, California
Completed 2006
264 Residences with 20% affordable
Client: Forest City Residential West
Contractor: Keller Builders
Structural engineer: Nabih Youssef Associates
MP engineer: VLA Engineers, Inc.
Electrical engineer: Vorgias Consulting
Landscape architect: Mia Lehrer + Associates

Blossom Plaza
Los Angeles, California
Completed: 2016
237 Residences with 20% affordable
Client: Forest City
Contractor: Morley Builders
Structural engineer: Englekirk Structural Engineers
MEP engineer: Donald F. Dickerson Associates
Landscape architect: Melendrez
Executive Architect: Togawa Smith Martin, Inc

LA Plaza Village
Los Angeles, California
Completed 2019
355 Residences with 20% affordable
Client: LA Plaza de Cultura y Artes Museum, County of Los Angeles, Cesar Chaves Foundation, Trammell Crow Company
Contractor: Morley Builders/ Benchmark Contractors
Structural engineer: John Labib & Associates
MEP engineer: Donald F. Dickerson Associates
Landscape architect: SWA
Interior Architect: Degen and Degen

Runway at Playa Vista
Playa Vista, California
Completed: 2015
217 Residences, 200,000 sq. ft. retail; 25,000 sq. ft. creative office
Client: Lincoln Property Company, Phoenix Property Company, Paragon Commercial Group
Construction Consultant: MBC Consultants, Inc
Contractor: Morley Builders
Structural engineer: Brockett Davis Drake, Inc
MEP engineer: Blum Consulting Engineers, Inc
Landscape architect: Rios Clemente Hale Studios
Interior Designer: Diana Wong Architecture + Interiors

College Station

Los Angeles, California
Completed: 2026
725 Residences
Client: Atlas Capital Group
Contractor: Bernards
Structural engineer: Englekirk Structural Engineers, Inc
MEP engineer: Donald F. Dickerson Associates
Landscape architect: Studio MLA

Citrus Commons

Sherman Oaks, California
Completed 2024
249 Residences
Client: IMT Residential
Contractor: IMT Residential
Structural engineer: Labib Funk & Associates
MEP engineer: Integral Group
Landscape architect: Duane Border

CRAFT

Opus One Winery

Oakville, California
Completed 1990
70,000 sq. ft.
Client: Opus One Winery
Construction management: L.E. Wentz Company
Engineers: The Bentley Company
Landscape architect: Royston Hanamoto Alley & Abbey

Opus One Winery Enhancements (Phase II)

Oakville, California
Completed 2019
58,000 sq. ft.
Client: Opus One Winery
Contractor: Wright Contracting
Structural engineer: Summit Engineering
MEP engineer: Costa Engineers; Summit Engineering
Finish, Furniture, & Fixtures: Joan Behnke and Associates, Inc

Aetna Springs Clubhouse and Resort

Pope Valley, California
Completed 2008
8,800 sq. ft.
Client: Criswell Radovan
Contractor: Turner Construction
Structural engineer: Parker Resnik
Interior design: Brayton Hughes Design Studios
Landscape architect: Smith+Smith

Byron Winery

Northern Santa Barbara County, California
Completed 1996
32,000 sq. ft.
Client: Robert Mondavi Winery
Contractor: BDM Construction Company, Inc.
Associate architect: Martinez & Associates
Structural engineer: Advanced Design Group, Inc.
Refrigeration engineer: G.J. Fehlhaber, P. E.
Electrical engineer: Gotham Light & Power
Landscape architect: Campbell & Campbell

Knife Pleat

Costa Mesa, California
Completed: 2019
5,000 sq. ft.
Client: Tony Esnault and Yassmin Sarmadi
Contractor: JRM Construction Management West
Structural engineer: Labib Funk and Associates
MEP engineer: Syska Hennessy Group, Inc.
Landscape architect: Duane Border

Sandy Lane Golf Clubhouse

St. James Parish, Barbados
Completed 2001
55,000 sq. ft.
Client: International Investment & Underwriting, Ltd.
Contractor:
Structural engineer: Nabih Youssef Associates
MP engineer: Leverage, Inc.
Electrical engineer: Kenderhall Enterprises Ltd.
Landscape architect: Tabora Tabora Blanco

Great Wall Winery

Hebei Province, China
Completed: 2019
147,000 sq. ft.
Client: China National Cereals, Oils and Foodstuffs Corporation (COFCC)
Contractor: Jiangsu Xingxia Construction Group Co, Ltd. (China)
Structural engineer: COFCC Wuxi Engineering Tech. Co. LTD.
MEP engineer: COFCC Wuxi Engineering Tech. Co. LTD.
Landscape architect: Duane Border Design

HOME

Wall House
Ojai, California
Completed: 2016
6,000 sq. ft.
Client: Private
Contractor: Minardos Group
Structural engineer: Nabih Youssef and Associates

Bridge House
Rutherford, California
Completed 1999
4,200 sq. ft.
Client: Private
Contractor: Bachor Construction
Structural engineer: Parker Resnick
MEP engineer: M B & A
Landscape architect: Jack Chandler & Associates

Box House
Saint Helena, California
Completed 1994
3,600 sq. ft.
Client: Private
Contractor: Bachor Construction
Structural engineer: Nabih Youssef Associates
MEP engineer: Myron Kim
Landscape architect: Jack Chandler & Associates

Frame House
Los Altos Hills, California
Completed 2001
6,800 sq. ft.
Client: Private
Contractor: Red Horse Constructors
Structural engineer: Lea & Sung Engineering
MEP engineer: Innovative Engineering Group, Inc.
Landscape architect: Nancy Goslee Power & Associates

Drum House
Malibu, California
Completed 2003
8,000 sq. ft.
Client: Private
Contractor: Peregrine Inc.
Structural engineer: Parker Resnick
MEP engineer: M B & A
Landscape architect: Campbell & Campbell

Inside/Outside House
Beverly Hills, California
Completed 2014
5,955 sq. ft.
Client: Private
Contractor: Winters + Schram Associates
Structural engineer: Nabih Youssef Associates
Mechanical engineer: JDA, Inc
Landscape architect: Duane Border Design

Larchmont Boulevard Townhouse
Los Angeles, California
Completed 2001
5,000 sq. ft.
Client: Private
Contractor: Minardos Builders
Structural engineer: Nabih Youssef Associates
MEP engineer: Innovative Engineering Group
Landscape architect: Judy M. Horton Garden Design

National Biscuit Company Loft
Los Angeles, California
Completed 2011
2,400 sq. ft.
Client: Private
Contractor: Minardos Builders

PROJECT SPONSORS

Aetna Preserve LLC
Apollo Real Estate Advisors, LP
All Saints' Episcopal Church
Amgen Inc.
Apple Inc
Atlas Capital Group
BaoDing City FuRui Landscape Co., Ltd.
Barker Pacific Group
Beacon Capital Partners
Bel-Air Country Club
Bio Marin Pharmaceutical Inc.
Brook Partners, Inc.
Byron Vineyard and Winery
C.C.A. Limited
California Institute of Technology
Catellus Development Corporation
CBRE, Inc.
Century City Realty LLC
Chateau Western Royal Spring Co., Ltd.
Chengdu Jin Tang LanGuang HeJun Property Development Co., Ltd.
Chengdu Wide Horizon New Town Development Co., Ltd.
China Foods Limited
Chris Radovan
Christ Catholic Cathedral Corporation
City of Beverly Hills
City of Los Angeles
City National Bank
Constellation Place, LLC
County of Los Angeles
Commonwealth Partners
Curtis School
Cushman & Wakefield of California, Inc.
Dallas Police and Fire Pension Systems
DanDong JinDi YingDa Real Estate Development Co., Ltd.
Dandong Nan-Tian-Yuan Real Estate Company, Ltd.
Dotterweich Carlson Mehner Design Inc.
Forest City Residential West, Inc.
Forest City Development Co.
Garden Lane Properties, LLC
Genentech, Inc.
GPI Companies
Hatch Mott MacDonald
Hines
HuaXia Great Wall Wine Co., Ltd.
IMT Residential
Jamison Properties
Jet Propulsion Laboratory
JMB Realty Corporation
JMI Realty
Laguna Beach Company
Lincoln Property Company
Los Altos Hills Estate
Los Angeles Unified School District
MacFarlane Partners
Mack Urban
Marlborough School
McCourt Group LLC
MDI-Miyama Development International
Metro-Goldwyn-Mayer Studios
Mitsui Fudosan America
Mr. Drew McCourt
Mr. Sandeep Reddy & Ms. Kavita Roye
Native American Cultural and Educational Authority
NBC Universal
Nolan Capital, Inc.
Opus One Winery
Pao Huei Development Co., Ltd.
Pao Huei Construction Co., Ltd
Playa Capital Company LLC
PT. Farpoint Realty Indonesia
QingDao MingHe Construction & Estate Development Co., Ltd.
Reality SF
Republic Metropolitan
Rising Realty Partners, LP
Robert Mondavi Winery
Sandstone Properties, Inc.
Silverstein Properties, Inc.
South Coast Plaza
State of California
State of Oklahoma
The Los Angeles Country Club
The Ratkovich Company
Tishman Speyer Properties
Trammell Crow Company
Transwestern
University of California, Berkeley
University of California, Irvine
University of California, Los Angeles
Venus Over Manhattan
Vista Canyon Ranch, LLC
Walt Disney Company
Walter J. Company
Warner Bros.
Wells Real Estate Fund
Unibail-Rodamco-Westfield
Tony Esnault, Yassmin Sarmadi

JOHNSON FAIN DESIGN TEAM

Shareefa Abdulsalam
Gevo Aelian
Nelson Almendarez
David Alpaugh
Larry Ball
Angela Barker
Yasaman Barmaki
Jocelyn Basseporte
Juan Carlos Begazo
Caroline Bell
Adrinee Bodakian
Paige Burke
Aron Carcamo
Adileni Caro
Helen Chen
Sherry Chen
Max Chirkov
Karen Choi
Hyeyoon Chung
Steve Chung
Rebecca Cohen
Tricia Converse
Arlene Cuevas
Weiyan Dai
Kersu Dalal
Angel De Romana
Ryan Del Poso
James (JED) Donaldson
Nastasja Dorandi
Shuangdi Dou
Kristine Edinchikyan
Natalie Egnatchik
William H. Fain, Jr.
Edwin Fang
Feryal Farahzad
Dana Fisher
Peter Flores
Garine Gabrielian
Shanoa Garcia
Linet Ghukasyan
Eric Giragosian
John Gralewski
Nicholas Guarna
Trina Gunther
Amira Hersi
Sapeer Hillel
Alexandra Holguin
Joy Huang
John Jackson
Daniel Janotta
Evan Jenkins
Kristina Johnson
Scott Johnson
Oleksandra Kazymirska
Gregory Keating
Aris Keshishian
Celine Khachatourian
Saba Khalili
Esra Kilickan
Paul Kim
Brian Knight
Dana Ladd
Amber Langlois
Craig Lawrence
Grace Lee
Leni Lee
Jeffrey Levy
Li Li
Xue Lin
Ethan Manaster
Abhijeet Mankar
Kristel Marquez
Richelle Leviste-Medina
Rouland Medina
Lex Moloney
Daniel Nay
Mark Owen
Andrew Palmer
Margie Parentela
David Park
Darnell Parker
Tigran Parsamyan
Luc Peltier
Sixto Pena
Chinh Pham
Alejandro Pijuan
Corey Pope
Isabel Portillo
Harold Ramirez
Raymond Rangel
Shahrzad Razi
Chris Roades
Taylor Sanderson
Joey Sandoval
Zlatan Sehovic
Alexander Sexsmith
Robert Shaffer
Keerthi Shekar
Aman Sheth
Juan Silva
Jillian Skelton
Dana Smith
Julia Smith
Boram Song
Jenifer Spangler
Suma Spina
Elsa Su
Matthew Sunseri
Anna Suo
Bahareh Tabatabaei
Crystal Tan
Travis Taylor
Bradley Thomas
Todd Thongeiam
Joshua Treiber
Gregory Verabian
Robert Villagomez
Nicole Villamin
Denis Vitoreli
Viviana Vivero
Wenlan Wang
Mehr Wani
Quincy Wargo
Bobby White
Eeechin Wong
Kevin Yan
Christian Yen
Sean Yun
Chunyan Zhang

PHOTOGRAPHY CREDITS

Page 1: Greg Keating
Page 2: Tom Bonner
Page 4: Tim Griffith (left image under "Tall")
(right image under "Culture")
Page 5: Paul Turang (left image under "Community")
Kirk Irwin (middle image under "Craft")
Tom Bonner (right image under "Home")
Page 6: Kyle Jeffers
Page 10: Craig Blackmon
Page 26: Tim Griffith
Page 28: Tim Griffith
Page 29: Tim Griffith
Page 30: Tim Griffith (Image Spread to Page 31)
Page 31: Tim Griffith (Same Image as Page 30)
Page 32: Tim Griffith
Page 33: Johnson Fain
Page 35: Terri Glanger (top and bottom)
Page 36: Tim Griffith
Page 37: Tom McConnell
Page 38: Kilograph
Page 39: Kilograph
Page 40: Kilograph 9
Page 42: Kilograph
Page 43: Kilograph
Page 44: Kilograph (top and bottom)
Page 47: Tim Griffith
Page 48: Tim Griffith
Page 49: Tim Griffith
Page 51: Pao Huei and HBA (top and bottom)
Page 52: Pao Huei and HBA (left and right)
Page 53: Tim Griffith
Page 54: Tim Griffith
Page 55: Tim Griffith
Page 56: Pao Huei Construction Co. Ltd. (top and bottom)
Page 57: Pao Huei Construction Co. Ltd.
Page 58: Pao Huei Construction Co. Ltd.
Page 62: Pao Huei Construction Co. Ltd.
Page 64: Pao Huei Construction Co. Ltd.
Page 65: Pao Huei Construction Co. Ltd.
Page 66: Pao Huei Construction Co. Ltd.
Page 68: Pao Huei Construction Co. Ltd.
Page 69: Pao Huei Construction Co. Ltd. (top and bottom)

Page 71: Pao Huei Construction Co. Ltd.
Page 72: Pao Huei Construction Co. Ltd.
Page 74: Pao Huei Construction Co. Ltd. (top and bottom)
Page 75: Pao Huei Construction Co. Ltd.
Page 76: Mario Wibowo (top and bottom)
Page 77: Mario Wibowo
Page 78: Fairpoint Realty (Image Spread to Page 79)
Page 79: Mario Wibowo
Page 81: Mario Wibowo
Page 82: Fairpoint Realty (left and right)
Page 84: Fairpoint Realty
Page 86: Craig Shimahara
Page 87: Craig Shimahara
Page 88: Craig Shimahara
Page 89: Craig Shimahara (bottom right)
Page 90: Craig Shimahara
Page 91: Craig Shimahara
Page 92: Craig Shimahara
Page 93: Craig Shimahara
Page 94: Craig Shimahara (bottom)
Page 95: Craig Shimahara
Page 96: Benny Chan/Fotoworks
Page 97: Benny Chan/Fotoworks
Page 98: Benny Chan/Fotoworks
Page 99: Benny Chan/Fotoworks
Page 100: Benny Chan/Fotoworks
Page 101: Benny Chan/Fotoworks (leftand right)
Page 102: Scott McDonald
Page 104: Scott McDonald
Page 108: Kansas State Historical Society (top and bottom)
Page 109: Scott McDonald
Page 110: Scott McDonald
Page 111: Scott McDonald left and right)
Page 112: Current Image- We cannot find a Photo Credit. (Left Small Image).
Replace with image FIRST AMERICANS MUSEUM 02 V2
Photo Credit:
Argo, Jim. Sac and Fox Pow Wow, photograph, July 15, 2002; (https://gateway.okhistory.org/ark:/67531/metadc1651758/: accessed September 27, 2022), The Gateway to Oklahoma History, https://gateway.okhistory.org; crediting Oklahoma Historical Society.
Page 113: Mel Willis Photography

Page 114: Craig Shimahara
Page 115: Tom Bonner
Page 116: Tom Bonner
Page 119: Tom Bonner
Page 120: Tom Bonner
Page 121: Tom Bonner (top and bottom)
Page 122: Tom Bonner
Page 123: Tom Bonner
Page 124: Erhard Pfeiffer
Page 126: Erhard Pfeiffer
Page 128: Erhard Pfeiffer (left and right)
Page 129: Richard Ross
Page 131: Michael O'Callahan
Page 132: Tim Griffith
Page 133: Michael O'Callahan
Page 134: Michael O'Callahan (top and bottom)
Page 135: Michael O'Callahan
Page 136: Craig Shimahara
Page 139: Craig Shimahara
Page 140: Johnson Fain
Page 143: Tim Griffith
Page 144: Tim Griffith (top and bottom)
Page 145: Tim Griffith
Page 146: Tim Griffith
Page 147: Tim Griffith (top and bottom)
Page 149: Benny Chan/Fotoworks
Page 150: Benny Chan/Fotoworks
Page 151: Tom Bonner (top and)bottom
Page 152: Benny Chan/Fotoworks (left and right)
Page 153: Benny Chan/Fotoworks
Page 154: Tim Griffith
Page 155: Tim Griffith
Page 156: Tim Griffith
Page 157: Tim Griffith (top and bottom)
Page 159: Benny Chan/Fotoworks
Page 161: Benny Chan/Fotoworks
Page 162: Hedrich Blessing Photographers
Page 163: Benny Chan/Fotoworks (top and bottom)
Page 164: Benny Chan/Fotoworks
Page 166: Benny Chan/Fotoworks
Page 167: Benny Chan/Fotoworks
Page 168: Benny Chan/Fotoworks

Page 169: Benny Chan/Fotoworks (top)
Page 169: Lawrence Anderson (bottom)
Page 170: Benny Chan/Fotoworks
Page 172: Benny Chan/Fotoworks
Page 173: Benny Chan/Fotoworks (top and bottom)
Page 174: Benny Chan/Fotoworks
Page 175: Benny Chan/Fotoworks (left and right)
Page 176: Eric Kieley
Page 178: Eric Kieley
Page 180: Eric Kieley
Page 181: Eric Kieley
Page 182: Eric Kieley (top and bottom)
Page 183: Eric Kieley (top and bottom)
Page 184: John Linden
Page 185: Eric Figge
Page 186: NO IMAGE
Page 187: Charles Lenoir
Page 188: Eric Figge
Page 189: Eric Figge
Page 190: Paul Turang
Page 192: Paul Turang Page 194: Eric Kieley
Page 195: Eric Kieley
Page 196: Trammel Crow
Page 198: Public Domain (bottom left). Graphic Designer Need To Check In Project Folder (Bottom Right Image)
Page 199: Collins Morley (top and bottom)
Page 200: Greg Keating
Page 201: Trammel Crow (top and bottom)
Page 202: Juan Tallo
Page 203: Jim Simmons
Page 204: Greg Keating
Page 205: Rober Meyers Studio
Page 206: Rober Meyers Studio
Page 207: Rober Meyers Studio
Page 208: Craig Shimahara
Page 211: Craig Shimahara (top and bottom)
Page 212: Craig Shimahara
Page 213: Craig Shimahara (bottom)
Page 214: Craig Shimahara (top and bottom)
Page 215: Craig Shimahara
Page 216: Craig Shimahara (top and bottom)
Page 218: Charles Callister, Jr.
Page 220: Tim Street Porter
Page 221: Mark Defeo
Page 222: Tim Street Porter
Page 223: Johnson Fain (top left and top right Image) Charles Callister, Jr. (bottom)
Page 224: Kyle JeffersPage 225: Charles Callister, Jr.
Page 226: Kyle Jeffers
Page 227: Kyle Jeffers (top and bottom))
Page 228: Tim Griffith
Page 229: Tim Griffith
Page 230: Bob Hughes (top)
Tim Griffith (bottom)
Page 231: Bob Hughes
Page 232: Erhard Pfeiffer
Page 233: Erhard Pfeiffer
Page 234: Erhard Pfeiffer
Page 235: Erhard Pfeiffer (left Image)
Page 236: Kirk Irwin
Page 237: Kirk Irwin
Page 239: Tom Bonner
Page 240: Tom Bonner
Page 242: Tom Bonner
Page 243: Tom Bonner (top and bottom)
Page 245: R.M.T. Photographics Ltd
Page 246: R.M.T. Photographics Ltd
Page 247: R.M.T. Photographics Ltd
Page 248: R.M.T. Photographics Ltd
Page 249: R.M.T. Photographics Ltd
Page 250: Qingyan Zhu
Page 251: Qingyan Zhu
Page 253: Qingyan Zhu
Page 254: Chang Tao
Page 255: Qingyan Zhu
Page 256: Sam Frost
Page 259: Tom Bonner
Page 260: Tom Bonner
Page 261: Tom Bonner (top and bottom)
Page 262: Tom Bonner
Page 263: Tom Bonner
Page 264: Tom Bonner
Page 265: Tom Bonner (top and bottom)
Page 266: Tim Griffith
Page 268: Sam Frost
Page 270: Tim Griffith
Page 271: Sam Frost
Page 272: Erhard Pfeiffer
Page 273: Tim Street Porter
Page 274: Erhard Pfeiffer
Page 275: Erhard Pfeiffer (top and bottom)
Page 276: Erhard Pfeiffer
Page 277: Erhard Pfeiffer
Page 278: Erhard Pfeiffer
Page 279. Erhard Pfeiffer
Page 280: Erhard Pfeiffer
Page 281: Erhard Pfeiffer
Page 282: Erhard Pfeiffer (left and right)
Page 283: Erhard Pfeiffer
Page 284: Tom Bonner
Page 287: Tom Bonner
Page 288: Tom Bonner
Page 289: Tom Bonner (left and right)
Page 290: Tom Bonner
Page 292: Tom Bonner (top and bottom)
Page 293: Tom Bonner
Page 294: Tom Bonner
Page 297: Russel Abraham
Page 298: Tim Street Porter
Page 299: Tim Street Porter
Page 300: Tim Street Porter (left and right)
Page 301: Tim Street Porter (left and right)
Page 303: Tom Bonner
Page 304: Tom Bonner
Page 305: Tom Bonner
Page 306: Tom Bonner
Page 307: Tom Bonner
Page 308: Johnson Fain

ACKNOWLEDGMENTS

We at Johnson Fain wish to thank all design team members over the years for their many valuable contributions. Work of this ambition and diversity requires high energy and collaboration. We thank our project sponsors and clients many of whom are real estate developers, museum directors, academicians, bioscientists, winemakers, and religious leaders. One of the many pleasures of being an architect is to be invited into communities and granted a window into other lives. We hope that we have done justice to translating their missions into physical space and materiality. Our work is not possible without the guidance and collaboration of our many creative colleagues: engineers, landscape architects, lighting designers, graphic artists, exhibition designers, and a host of specialty consultants. They bring totality to the process of design. We thank Kurt Hauser for what we feel is an intelligent and elegant book design and Michael Webb for the insightful Foreword. Michael has long been a prolific writer on matters of design and architecture and is equally knowledgeable about Southern Californian and global events. We thank ORO Editions for overseeing the publication of this work. They have exemplified professionalism and craft throughout the predictably arduous process of creating such a book. In the studio at Johnson Fain, we thank Jed Donaldson, Trisha Converse, Mark Owen, Richelle Leviste, Amira Hersi, Nicholas Guarna, Ryan Del Poso and Esra Kilickan for many and varied contributions to this monograph.

ORO Editions
Publishers of Architecture, Art, and Design
Gordon Goff: Publisher

www.oroeditions.com
info@oroeditions.com

Published by ORO Editions

Library of Congress Control Number: 2022923666

Author: Scott Johnson
Book Design: Kurt Hauser
Pre-press assitance: CircularStudio
Project Manager: Jake Anderson
10 9 8 7 6 5 4 3 2 1 First Edition

ISBN: 978-1-957183-44-2

Color Separations and Printing: ORO Group Inc.
Printed in Hong Kong

ORO Editions makes a continuous effort to minimize the overall carbon footprint of its publications. As part of this goal, ORO, in association with Global ReLeaf, arranges to plant trees to replace those used in the manufacturing of the paper produced for its books. Global ReLeaf is an international campaign run by American Forests, one of the world's oldest nonprofit conservation organizations. Global ReLeaf is American Forests' education and action program that helps individuals, organizations, agencies, and corporations improve the local and global environment by planting and caring for trees.